Michael Price

OFFICE
2007

in
easy steps

In easy steps is an imprint of Computer Step
Southfield Road · Southam
Warwickshire CV47 0FB · United Kingdom
www.ineasysteps.com

Notice of Liability
Every effort has been made to ensure that this book contains accurate
and current information. However, Computer Step and the author
shall not be liable for any loss or damage suffered by readers as a
result of any information contained herein.

Trademarks
Microsoft® and Windows® are registered trademarks of Microsoft
Corporation. All other trademarks are acknowledged as belonging to
their respective companies.

Printed and bound in the United Kingdom

ISBN-13 978-1-84078-344-5
ISBN-10 1-84078-344-3

Contents

Calculations   67

Manage Data   85

Presentations   107

7 Office Extras 127

8 Email 145

9 Time Management 165

10 Manage Files   187

11 Up to Date and Secure   203

12 Where Next?   219

Index   233

1 Introducing Office 2007

This chapter discusses the latest version of Microsoft Office with its new style of user interface. It identifies the range of editions and outlines the requirements for installation. Also covered are the process of starting applications, the main features shared by Office applications, a summary of the new Office document types and compatibility with the older versions.

Microsoft Office 2007

Microsoft Office is a productivity suite of applications that share common features and approaches. There have been numerous versions, including Office 95, Office 97, Office 2000, Office XP (also called Office 2002) and Office 2003. The latest version, released in January 2007, is Microsoft Office 2007.

There are various editions with particular combinations of products. The Standard edition contains these applications:

- Excel 2007 — Spreadsheet and data manager
- PowerPoint 2007 — Presentations and slide shows
- Outlook 2007 — Electronic mail and diary
- Word 2007 — Text editor and word processor
- Office Tools — Diagnostics and image utilities

The Professional edition of Office contains all of these products with the addition of some business-oriented applications:

- Access 2007 — Database manager
- Accounting Express 2007 — USA only
- Business Contact Manager — Extension to Outlook 2007
- Publisher 2007 — Professional document creation

The Ultimate edition of Office contains all of Professional, plus additional products including:

- InfoPath 2007 — Database manager
- OneNote 2007 — For taking notes

There's a Home and Student edition, which is like Standard, but with the OneNote application instead of Outlook. This edition is very good value, and you don't have to be a student. To illustrate the relative costs, the prices in the USA are:

Edition	Full	Upgrade	Licenses
Home and Student	$149	n/a	Up to three PCs
Standard	$399	$239	
Professional	$499	$329	One or two PCs
Ultimate	$679	$539	

Don't forget

New PCs may come with Office 2007 Basic edition, which is like Standard but without PowerPoint. See page 220 for details of all the editions of Office.

Don't forget

Qualifying Microsoft products for upgrade are Works 6.0–10, Works suite 2000–2006 or later, any 2000–2007 Office program or suite and any Office XP suite except Office XP Student and Teacher.

Ribbon Technology

Whichever edition you have, the most notable feature of Office 2007 is the entirely new graphical user interface based on the Ribbon technology. This replaces the menus and toolbars that were the essence of all previous versions.

This shows the Ribbon in Word 2007, with the Home tab selected. This tab usually displays six groups associated with basic document creation - Clipboard, Font, Paragraph, Styles and Editing. Some additional contextual tabs appear when appropriate. Each group contains a set of related commands and icons.

The Ribbon contains command buttons and icons, organized in a set of tabs, each containing groups of commands associated with specific functions. The purpose is to make the relevant features more intuitive and more readily available. This allows you to concentrate on the tasks you want to perform rather than the details of how you will carry out the activities.

Some tabs appear only when certain objects are selected. These are known as contextual tabs and provide functions that are specific to the selected object, for example an inserted image:

This shows the Picture Tools Format group which is added to the Home tab in Word 2007, when you select an inserted picture.

The new user interface also features extended ScreenTips that can contain images and links to more help, as well as text. The tips are displayed when you move the mouse pointer over a command, and they describe what the commands are able to do.

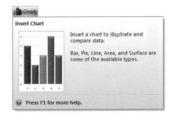

What's Needed

To use Microsoft Office 2007, you will need at least the following components in your computer:

- 500 MHz processor

- 256 MB memory

- 1.5–3.0 GB available disk space

- CD-ROM or DVD drive

- 1024×768-resolution monitor

- Windows Vista or Windows XP with SP2

Some functions impose more stringent requirements, for example:

- 512 MB memory for Outlook Instant Search

- 1.0 GB memory for Word grammar and contextual spelling

- Internet connection for online help

If your computer is running Windows Vista, you'll find that the system specifications already meet or exceed requirements for Office 2007. You'll also find that the Office 2007 user interface coordinates well with the visual style of Windows Vista and Aero.

Hot tip

The larger amount of disk space is required for the more comprehensive editions of Office 2007, such as Professional or Ultimate.

Beware

These are the minimum requirements. A higher-speed processor with additional memory is the preferred configuration.

10

Don't forget

The illustrations in this book are usually based on Office Ultimate edition running under Windows Vista Ultimate. However, the tasks shown generally apply to any edition or operating environment.

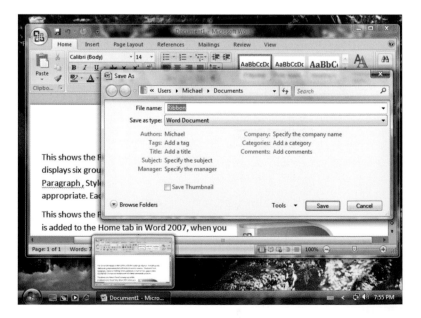

Installing Office 2007

If you've purchased a new copy of Office 2007, you will need to install it onto your computer. Insert the supplied CD or DVD, enter the 25-character product key and accept the terms and conditions. Follow the prompts to complete the installation.

1 Select Install Now to accept the default settings

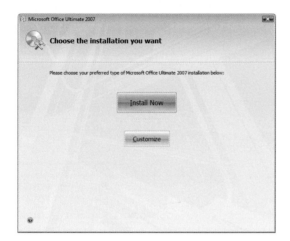

2 Select Customize to choose how items are installed, then click a component and choose "Run all from My Computer" to include all the extras

3 Select Not Available to exclude the selected component

Start an Application

When you have installed Office 2007, a new folder of shortcuts will be added to the Start Menu.

1 Select Start, All Programs

2 Select Microsoft Office to display all the installed applications

3 Select Microsoft Office Tools to display the various utilities

4 Select the application that you wish to run, for example Word 2007

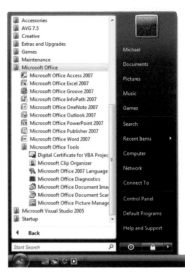

When you start any Office application, you are reminded that you must activate your installation to fully enable all the features.

5 You can activate your copy of Office 2007 over the Internet or by telephone

The Application Window

When you start an Office application such as Excel, PowerPoint or Word, the program window is displayed with a blank document named book1, presentation1 or document1 respectively.

Office button   Quick Access toolbar   Document name   Tabs   Minimize/Restore/Close

Ribbon

Commands and icons (display lists or galleries)

Launch button (show dialog box)

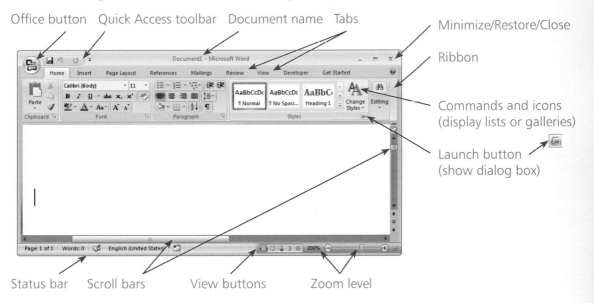

Status bar   Scroll bars   View buttons   Zoom level

Applications such as Access and Publisher don't open a blank document but instead offer a selection of predefined application document layouts. For Publisher, these include brochures, business cards and calendars. Blank document layouts are also available.

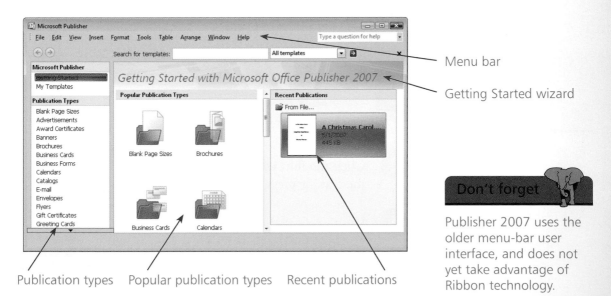

Menu bar

Getting Started wizard

Publication types   Popular publication types   Recent publications

Publisher 2007 uses the older menu-bar user interface, and does not yet take advantage of Ribbon technology.

Live Preview

With applications that use the Ribbon, you can see the effect on your document of formatting options such as fonts and styles, by simply pointing to the proposed change. For example, to see font formatting changes:

 Highlight the text that you may wish to change, and select the Home tab

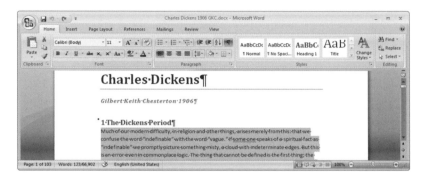

 Click the arrow next to the Font box and move the mouse pointer over the fonts you'd like to preview

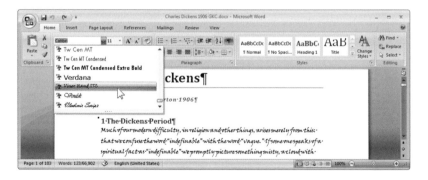

 Click the font you want, to actually apply the change to the text, or press Escape to finish viewing font options

 You can similarly preview the alternatives provided for the Font Size, the Font Color and the Text Highlight Color options

...cont'd

Live Preview is available for paragraph format options (e.g. bullets, numbering and shading) and for styles.

 1 Highlight the text that you may wish to change, and select the Home tab

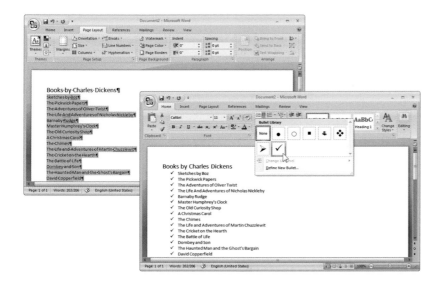

2 Display the list of paragraph options, and move the mouse pointer over any that you want to preview

3 Display the list of styles (with no text selected) and preview the complete document in a variety of styles

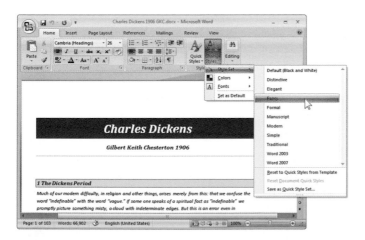

Don't forget

This facility is not available in Excel, which does not offer the Paragraph group.

Hot tip

The option will be previewed for the paragraph where the pointer is currently located, if no text has been selected.

Don't forget

You can turn off Live Preview for individual applications. Click the Office button, select the application Options, click Popular and clear the Enable Live Preview box.

Top options for working with Excel

☑ Show Mini Toolbar on selection ⓘ
☑ Enable Live Preview ⓘ
☐ Show Developer tab in the Ribbon ⓘ

Save the Document

You'll use the appropriate commands on the Ribbon for each particular application, to create and amend the application document. You should save the document periodically, to avoid the possibility of losing the work you've done.

Hot tip

See page 26 for an example of creating a Word document, and page 70 for an Excel workbook.

Beware

A name such as book1 or book2 assigned to a blank document is a temporary name and a permanent name must be provided when the document is first saved.

16

 1 To save the document, click the Office button and select Save

2 For a document not yet named and saved, the Save As dialog opens and you can provide a name (or use the suggested name)

Hot tip

For applications such as Access or Publisher that use the previous user interface, you'd select File, Save.

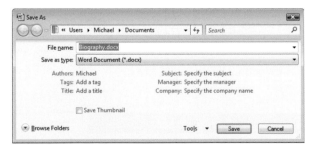

 3 On subsequent Saves, the document will be written to disk without any further action needed

Working With the Ribbon

The Ribbon takes up a significant amount of the window space, especially when you have a lower-resolution display. To hide it:

17

 Right-click the tab row and select Minimize the Ribbon

| Customize Quick Access Toolbar... |
| Show Quick Access Toolbar Below the Ribbon |
| Minimize the Ribbon |

 The Office button, Quick Access toolbar and tab row will still be displayed while the Ribbon is minimized

Hot tip

When the application window is reduced below a certain width or depth, the Ribbon may get automatically hidden, along with the Office button, the tabs row and the Quick Access bar.

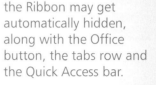

The Ribbon reappears temporarily when you click one of the tabs, so you can select the required command

 Alternatively, press and release the Alt key to display keyboard shortcuts for the tabs

Hot tip

Repeat step 1 to redisplay the Ribbon.

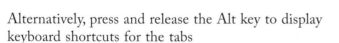

Don't forget

Hold down the Alt key and press the keys in sequence, for a two-letter shortcut such as PW (Watermark). Press Esc to go back up a level.

Press Alt + shortcut key, for example Alt+P to select Page Layout, and display the Ribbon and shortcuts for that tab

Quick Access Toolbar

The Quick Access toolbar contains a set of commands that are independent of the selected tab. There are initially four buttons:

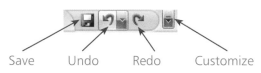

Save   Undo   Redo   Customize

Hot tip

The Save As dialog will open the first time you click Save for a new document (see page 30).

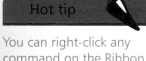

Hot tip

You can right-click any command on the Ribbon and select Add to Quick Access Toolbar.

 1 Click the Save button to write the current contents of the application document to the disk drive

2 Click Undo to reverse the last action, click Redo to re-apply, and click the arrow to select several actions

3 Click the Customize button to add or remove icons using the list of popular commands

 4 Click More Commands to display the full list of commands, then add and remove entries as desired

Don't forget

You can click the Office button, then click the application Options, and select Customize to display this dialog.

Office Document Types

The objects you create using the Office applications will be office documents of various types, including:

- Formatted text and graphics   Word document
- Flyers and brochures   Publisher publication
- Spreadsheets and data lists   Excel worksheet
- Presentations and slide shows   PowerPoint presentation

Each item will be a separate file. By default, these will be saved in the Documents folder for your username (logon ID).

1 To show the entries currently stored in your folder, click Start and select Documents from the list

2 Click Views, and choose Details to show the file information, including the date modified, the size and the file type

Hot tip

The files will be stored in My Documents for Office applications running under Windows XP (see page 189).

Don't forget

You can specify a different folder or create a new folder for particular documents.

Name	Date modified	Type	Size	Tags
EricCitations	5/1/2007 10:31 AM	Microsoft Office Access 2007 Database	420 KB	
Bibliography	5/1/2007 6:56 AM	Microsoft Office Excel Worksheet	11 KB	
Charles Dickens Resources	5/1/2007 9:50 AM	Microsoft Office OneNote Section	2,156 KB	
Dickens	5/1/2007 9:41 AM	Microsoft Office PowerPoint Presentation	203 KB	
A Christmas Carol	5/1/2007 9:06 AM	Microsoft Office Publisher Document	445 KB	
Biography	5/1/2007 6:19 AM	Microsoft Office Word Document	16 KB	

EricCitations   Date modified: 5/1/2007 10:31 AM
Microsoft Office Access 2007 Database   Size: 420 KB
Date created: 5/1/2007 10:26 AM

Note that in some applications, groups of related items will be stored together in a specially structured file. For example:

- Data tables, queries and reports   Access database
- Messages, contacts and tasks   Outlook folders
- Notes and reminders   OneNote folders

File Extensions

To see the file extensions associated with these document types:

Don't forget

For Windows XP, you'd choose Appearance and Themes from the Control Panel and then select Folder Options.

1 Select Start, Control Panel, click Appearance and Personalization and then click Folder Options

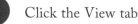

2 Click the View tab

3 Search through the list of "Advanced settings" and clear "Hide extensions for known file types"

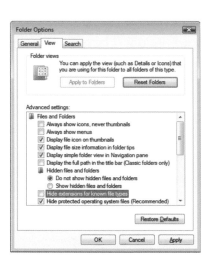

4 Click OK to apply the change to all folders

5 The file type will be shown along with the file name, whichever folder view you choose

Don't forget

Files saved in the Office 2007 format use new file extensions e.g. .docx and .xlsx. This is the OpenXML file format.

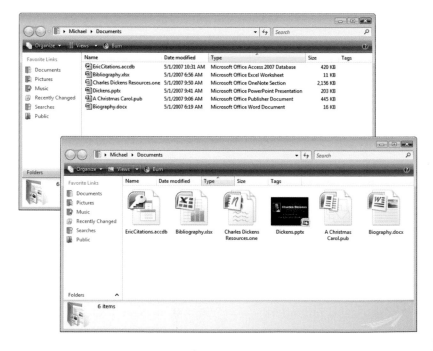

Compatibility Mode

Office 2007 will open documents created in previous versions of Office applications, for example .doc (Word), .xls (Excel) and .ppt (PowerPoint).

1 Click the Office button and select Open, then click the down arrow for document type to list the types supported

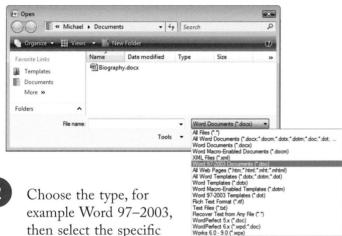

2 Choose the type, for example Word 97–2003, then select the specific document name

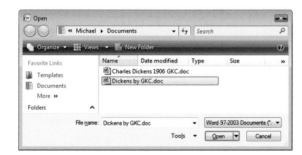

3 The document will be opened in Compatibility Mode

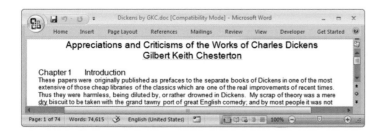

Hot tip

You may need to save documents in Compatibility Mode, as those you wish to share files with may not have Office 2007.

21

Don't forget

Compatibility Mode prevents the use of new or enhanced features, so the document can be used by systems with the older applications.

Convert to Office 2007

If you have opened a document in Compatibility Mode, you can convert it to Office 2007.

 1 Click the Office button and select Convert

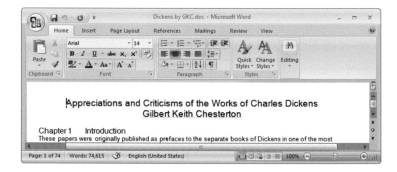

Microsoft Office Word

This action will convert the document to the newest file format. The layout of the document may change.

Converting allows you to use all the new features of Word and reduces the size of your file. This document will be replaced by the converted version.

☐ Do not ask me again about converting documents

Tell Me More...   OK   Cancel

 2 Click OK to confirm you want to update the document, and the compatibility restriction will be removed

Dickens by GKC.doc - Microsoft Word

Home Insert Page Layout References Mailings Review View

Appreciations and Criticisms of the Works of Charles Dickens
Gilbert Keith Chesterton

Chapter 1   Introduction
These papers were originally published as prefaces to the separate books of Dickens in one of the most

Page: 1 of 74   Words: 74,615   English (United States)   100%

 3 Now, to replace the original file, click the Office button and Save, or click Save on the Quick Access toolbar

 4 To retain the original document and create a new document in Office 2007 format, click the Office button and select Save As

Save As

« Users ▶ Michael ▶ Documents   ▼ ↵   Search

File name: Dickens by GKC.docx

Save as type: Word Document (*.docx)

Authors: Michael Price   Manager: Specify the manager
Tags: Add a tag   Company: Queensmead
Title: Gilbert Keith Chesterton   Categories: Add a category
Subject: Specify the subject   Comments: Add comments

☐ Save Thumbnail

Browse Folders   Tools ▼   Save   Cancel

Solving Problems

If you suffer abnormal terminations with any Office applications, Office Diagnostics will help identify and resolve the problem.

 1 Select Start, All Programs, Microsoft Office, Microsoft Office Tools and then click Microsoft Office Diagnostics

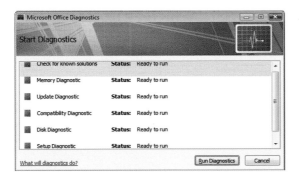

 2 Click the Run Diagnostics button to start the process

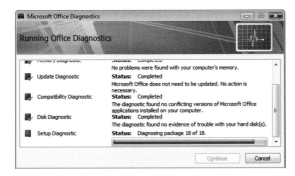

 3 The diagnostics run automatically and report the findings

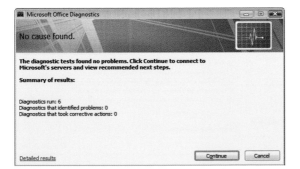

Hot tip

You can also start the diagnostics from the Office application. Click the Office button and select Options, Resources and Diagnose.

Diagnose

Beware

The tests take up to 15 minutes and you should avoid using the system while they are running.

23

Hot tip

The information that is displayed will depend on the findings of your diagnostic check. In this example there are no current problems, so all the tests complete successfully.

...cont'd

4 After completing Office Diagnostics, click Continue to go to Office Online for further information

5 This may tell you Update Diagnostics were unable to run

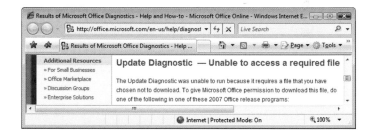

Hot tip

The first time you run the diagnostics, you may need to download a file to enable access to the results.

6 To enable the Update Diagnostic, click the Office button, select Options, click Trust Center, Trust Center Settings and Privacy Options and choose to download the file that helps assess problems

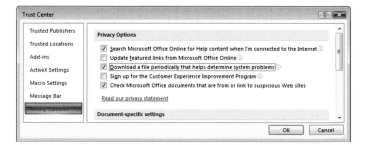

Beware

You may have to wait for several days before this file gets downloaded and Update Diagnostic get added to the list of Office Diagnostics.

2 Create Word Documents

This covers the basics of word processing using the Word application in Office 2007. It covers entering, selecting and copying text, saving and autosaving, and proofing the text. It looks at the use of styles to structure the document, and at adding document features such as pictures, columns and word counts. It also discusses ways of creating tables, the use of Paste Special and the facilities for printing.

Start a Word Document

1 Right-click an empty space in a folder (e.g. Documents) and select New, Microsoft Office Word Document

Hot tip

The document will be named New Microsoft Office Word Document (though you can over-type this with a more relevant name). Double-click the file icon to open the document in Word.

2 A blank document, temporarily named Document1, will be started when you open Word (see page 12)

Don't forget

Word keeps count of all documents created during the session, and allocates the next available number.

3 If Word is already open, click the Office button, select Open, choose the blank document and click to create a document, named, for example, Document2

Enter Text

1 Click on the page, and type the text that you want. If the text is longer than a single line, Word automatically starts the new line for you

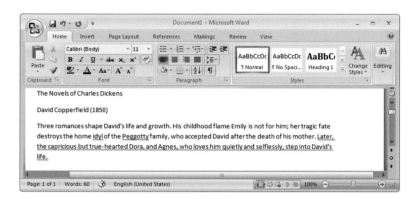

2 Press Enter when you need to start a new line or paragraph

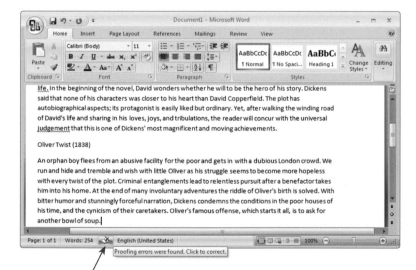

3 Proofing errors may be detected as indicated by the wavy underscores – red (spelling) or green (grammar). Click the button on the status bar to correct them one by one, or correct them all at the same time, when you've typed in the whole document (see page 31)

Hot tip

You can copy and paste text from other sources such as web pages. Use Paste Special (see page 43) to avoid copying styles and formats along with the text.

Don't forget

You may see blue underscores to indicate contextual spelling errors (misused words).

Select and Copy Text

It's necessary to select text for many purposes in Word, so it's not surprising that there are numerous ways to select just the amount of text you require, using the mouse or the keyboard as preferred. To select the entire document use one of these options:

1 Select the Home tab, click Select in the Editing group and then click the Select All command

2 Move the mouse pointer to the left of any text until it turns into a right-pointing arrow, then triple-click

3 Press the shortcut keys Ctrl+A

There are many mouse and keyboard options for selecting a piece of text in the body of the document. For example:

1 Double-click anywhere in a word to select the word

2 Hold down Ctrl and click anywhere in a sentence to select the whole sentence

3 To select a portion of text, click at the start, hold down the left mouse button and drag the pointer over the text

Hot tip

A single click selects just the line of text to the right of the arrow, and a double click selects the whole paragraph

28

Don't forget

Using the keyboard, you can press F8 to turn on Selection Mode, then press F8 once again to select the word nearest the insertion point, twice to select the sentence, three times for the paragraph and four times for the document.

...cont'd

You can use text selection in combination with the Clipboard tools to copy or move parts of the text. For example:

 1 Select a section of text using the mouse

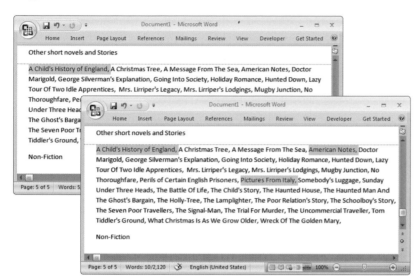

 **Don't forget**

You can use the keyboard shortcuts Ctrl+C (copy), Ctrl+X (cut) and Ctrl+V (paste) instead of the Clipboard buttons.

2 Hold down the Ctrl key and select additional pieces of text, then select Home and click Cut in the Clipboard group

Hot tip

Click the Copy button if you want to duplicate the text rather than move it.

3 Click the position where the text is required and then select Home and click the Paste button

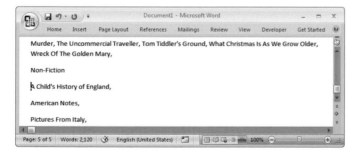

 **Don't forget**

The Paste Special option in the Clipboard group (see page 43) allows you to copy text without replicating its formatting.

4 If you've copied several pieces of text, you may need to delete the end-of-line characters to join them up

Save the Document

When you are building a document, Word will periodically save a copy of the document, just in case a problem should arise. This minimizes the amount of text you may need to re-enter. This feature is known as AutoRecover. To check the settings:

 Click the Office button, select Word Options and click the Save option

By default, Word will save AutoRecover information every ten minutes, but you can change the frequency.

To make an immediate save of your document:

 Click the Save button on the Quick Access toolbar

 The first time, you'll be prompted to confirm the location, the file name and the document type that you want to use

 On subsequent occasions, the copy of the document on hard disk will be updated immediately, without any interaction required

Beware

If the system terminates abnormally, any data entered since the last AutoRecover operation will be lost.

Don't forget

You can also select Office, Save As to specify a new location, name or document type.

Correct Proofing Errors

When you've entered all the text, you can correct proofing errors.

 1 Press Ctrl+Home to go to the start of the document, then select the Review tab and click Spelling & Grammar

Hot tip

The spelling check will commence from the current location of the typing cursor, if you don't relocate to the start of the document.

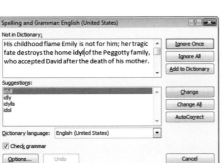

2 For spelling errors, choose the correct word and click Change

Make sure that the appropriate dictionary is enabled for the document you are checking.

3 For terms or proper names, select Ignore All or (if the name is used often) Add to Dictionary

4 Grammar and style errors are less definitive, so you must decide about each suggestion on its merits

Don't forget

Each error is presented in turn (unless previous choices such as Ignore All cause the error to get cleared), until the spelling check is complete.

31

Change Proofing Settings

Don't forget

You can make changes to the settings for the spelling checks and for the grammar and style checks.

1 Click the Office button, select Word Options and then select the Proofing option

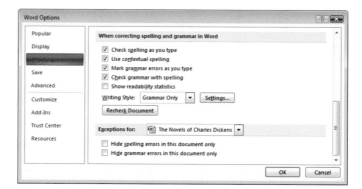

2 Some settings, such as "Ignore words in uppercase" and "Flag repeated words", apply to all the Office applications

Hot tip

If you'd rather not use the grammar checker, clear the boxes for "Mark grammar errors as you type" and "Check grammar with spelling". Alternatively, you can hide errors in the particular document.

3 Some settings, such as "Check spelling as you type" and "Mark grammar errors as you type", are specific to the particular Office application

Suggestions are:

seen
see
Where

4 The new contextual spelling checker in Word identifies words that are spelled correctly but used in the wrong context, and suggests alternative words that might be more appropriate

Apply Styles

1 Click the main heading and select Style Heading 1

 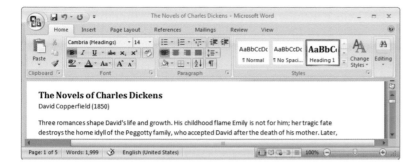

2 Click one of the subsidiary headings and select Heading 2

3 Click in the text paragraph and select No Spacing

 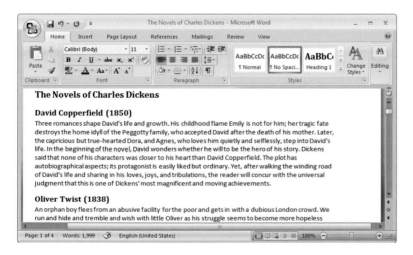

Outline View

When you have structured the document using headings, you can view it as an outline:

1 Select the View tab and click the Outline button to switch to Outline view and enable the Outlining tab

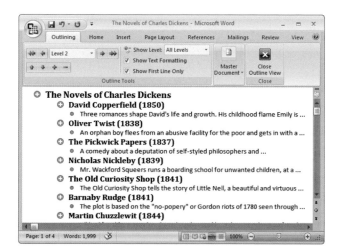

2 In the Outline Tools group click the box labelled Show First Line Only, so that you can see more entries at once

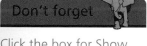
This makes it easier for you to identify any entries that are out of order. In this example the entries for David Copperfield and Oliver Twist are out of chronological sequence.

Outline view also makes it easy for you to reposition selected entries.

1 Click the arrow next to Show Level, and choose Level 2

2 Click an entry, e.g. David Copperfield, and click the down arrow to move it

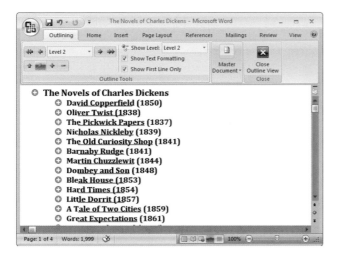

3 The selected entry, with all its subsidiary levels and text, will move one row for each click of the arrow button

Don't forget

This will display the selected level and all higher levels.

Don't forget

The Outline tools also provide buttons that allow you to promote or demote selected entries.

Hot tip

You can click the + symbol next to an entry to select it and then drag it to the required location.

Insert a Picture

Hot tip

You can insert a variety of items into your document, including pictures, tables, headers and footers, WordArt and symbols.

1 Position the typing cursor at the location where the item is required, inserting a blank line if desired

2 Select the Insert tab and click the appropriate icon or command, for example Picture (in the Illustrations group)

3 Locate the file for the picture, and click the Insert button

Don't forget

The picture will be added to the document, in line with the text. Note the addition of the Picture Tools Format tab.

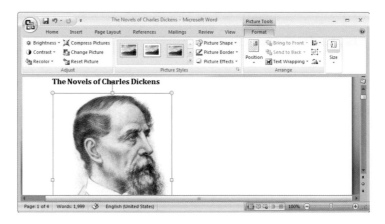

...cont'd

You can adjust the position of the picture on the page of text.

1 Click the Position button in the Arrangements group and move the pointer over the buttons

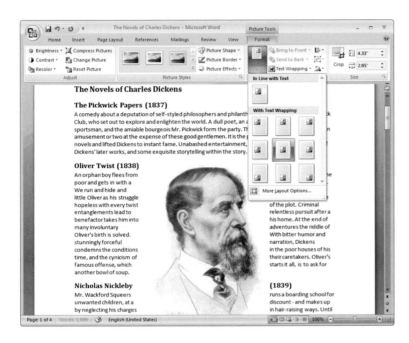

2 A live preview will be displayed. Click the appropriate button for the position you prefer

3 Click the up or down arrow on the height to adjust the size of the picture. The width is changed proportionally

Page Layout

The Page Layout tab allows you to control how the document contents are placed on the page, by just clicking one of the function commands in the Page Setup group.

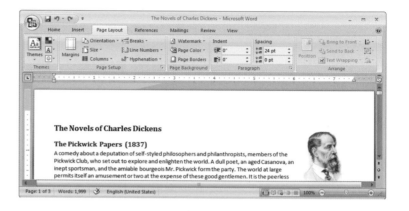

1 Click the Orientation command to select Portrait or Landscape

2 Click the Size command to select the paper size from the list, or click More Paper Sizes to show other choices, including the Custom Size option

3 Click the Margins command to choose one of the predefined setups, or click Custom Margins to display the Page Setup dialog and enter specific values

Display in Columns

1 Select the text you wish to put into columns, click the Page Layout tab and select Columns from Page Setup

2 Choose the number of columns required

3 Click anywhere in the body text, select the Home tab, click Select, Select Text with Similar Formatting and then click the Justify button

Choose Justify for the paragraph text to help give the document the appearance of newspaper columns. Click in the main title text and then choose Center to position the title over the three columns.

Word Count

If you are preparing a document for a publication, such as a club magazine, you may need to keep track of the number of words you've produced. Word 2007 makes this easy to do.

Hot tip

You can also display the details by selecting the Review tab and clicking Word Count in the Proofing group.

1 At any time, you can view the latest word count on the status bar

2 Click the word count to display further details of the content

Don't forget

The display of readability statistics is controlled via the Proofing settings (see page 32).

For more information, turn on Readability Statistics, which assess the complexity of the contents.

3 Select the Review tab and click Spelling & Grammar in the Proofing group

4 After the spelling check, the statistics are displayed

Create a Table

To specify a table in your document:

 Click the point where you want the table, then click the Insert tab and select Table

 Move the pointer over the Insert Table area to select the number of rows and columns, then click to confirm

Book Title	Published	Lines of Text	Total Words	Variety of Words
The Pickwick Papers	1837	30203		

Enter the required contents. Press the Tab key to move to the next cell in the table

Book Title	Published	Lines of Text	Total Words	Variety of Words
The Pickwick Papers	1837	30203	309327	14850
Oliver Twist	1838	14998	162760	10321
Nicholas Nickleby	1839	29642	328994	14579
The Old Curiosity Shop	1841	18284	221854	12024

Hot tip

You'll see previews of the indicated table sizes, as you move the pointer across the Insert Table area.

Don't forget

Press the arrow keys to navigate around the table. Click and drag a separator line to adjust the width of a column.

Convert Text

If you already have the text that's needed for the table, taken from another document perhaps, you can convert the text into a table.

Place two separator characters consecutively, to indicate an empty cell. Paragraph marks separate the data for the individual rows.

 1 Make sure that the cell entries are separated by a tab mark or some other unique character

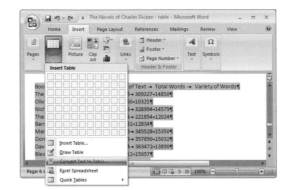

Click "Autofit to contents" to adjust the column widths to match the data in those cells.

 2 Highlight the text, select the Insert tab and then click Table, Convert Text to Table

3 Specify your particular separation character and then click OK

 4 The table will be created with the data inserted into the relevant cells

From the Table Tools Layout tab, you can merge cells and insert or delete rows and columns in the table.

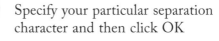

Book Title	Published	Lines of Text	Total Words	Variety of Words
The Pickwick Papers	1837	30203	309327	14850
Oliver Twist	1838	14998	162760	10321
Nicholas Nickleby	1839	29642	328994	14579
The Old Curiosity Shop	1841	18284	221854	12024
Barnaby Rudge	1841	21388	259882	12834
Martin Chuzzlewit	1844	29880	345528	15350
Dombey and Son	1848	30933	357890	15032
David Copperfield	1850	30264	363472	13890
Bleak House	1853	30684	362012	15057
Hard Times	1854	9173	105607	8741
Little Dorrit	1857	28973	344932	14786
A Tale of Two Cities	1859	12810	138150	9732
Great Expectations	1861	15906	189173	10733
Our Mutual Friend	1865	33143	333784	14979
The Mystery of Edwin Drood	1870	11840	95944	9103

Paste Special

To copy the text without including its formatting and graphics:

 1 Highlight the text you want, then right-click the selected area and click the Copy command

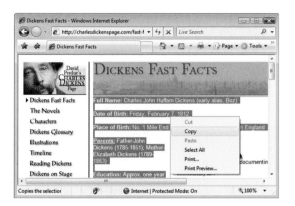

 2 Click in the document where the text is to appear, select the Home tab, and click the arrow below the Paste button

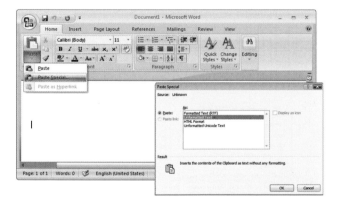

3 Click Paste Special and choose Paste, Unformatted Text

Hot tip

When you copy information from other documents or from web pages, the text may include graphics, formatting and colors that are inappropriate for your document.

Beware

Graphical information won't be copied, even if it has the appearance of text (as with the "Dickens Fast Facts" title of the text being copied for this example).

43

Don't forget

The copied text will inherit the format of that part of the document where you clicked before carrying out the paste operation.

Print Document

To print a document from within Word:

 1 Click the Office button and select Print (or press Ctrl+P)

2 Select the printer to use, adjust options such as the specific pages to be printed print and the number of copies required, then click OK to begin the printing

 3 To print a single copy of the whole document on the default printer, click Office, click the arrow next to Print and then select Quick Print

3 Complex Documents

Microsoft Word can be used to create and edit more complex documents such as booklets and brochures. This chapter covers importing text, inserting illustrations, creating tables of contents and illustrations. It shows how templates can be used to help create documents. It also introduces Publisher, the Office application that is specifically designed for desktop publishing.

Start a Booklet

To illustrate some of the facilities available for creating and organizing complex documents, we'll go through the process of importing and structuring the text for a booklet. In this example we use *A Christmas Carol* by Charles Dickens.

 Start by typing the book title, author and chapter names

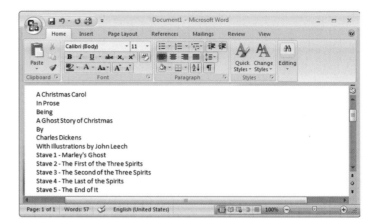

46

 Set the language. This is a UK English book, so press Ctrl+A to select the text, click the Language button on the status bar and pick English (United Kingdom)

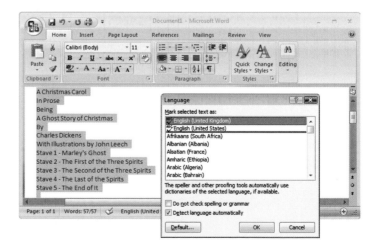

 Click Save on the Quick Access toolbar, and provide a name for the document, or accept the suggested name

Choose Page Arrangement

Before adding more text, set the paper size and the margins.

1 Select the Page Layout tab, and click Size to choose paper size, e.g. Letter

2 Click Margins and choose the Custom Margins option

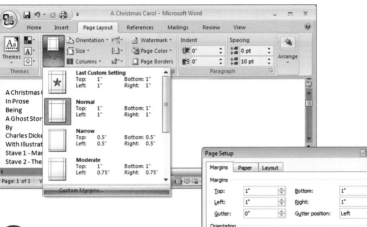

3 From the Page Setup dialog, in the Pages section, select "Multiple pages", "Book fold"

4 Specify the number of sheets per booklet (in multiples of 4 up to 40) or choose All to assemble the document as a single booklet

For a book or brochure, you may want to arrange the pages in the form of booklets.

The orientation changes to landscape, and you get four pages of the document on each piece of paper (printed on both sides). A four-sheet booklet, for example, would be printed as:

Front

Back

Create the Structure

1 Highlight the text for the chapter titles

In keeping with the "Christmas carol" theme, the chapters in this book are known as Staves.

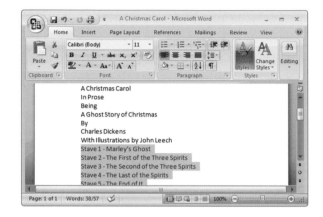

2 Click the Home tab and select Quick Styles, Heading 1

Don't forget

The formatting changes center the chapter titles over the text that will be inserted (see page 50).

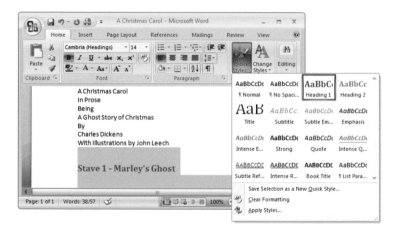

3 With the chapter titles still selected, click the Center button in the Paragraph group

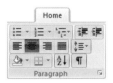

Hot tip

Steps 4 to 6 illustrate how you can use Find and Replace to insert special characters, such as line breaks.

4 To replace hyphens by line breaks in the chapter titles, click the Editing button and select Replace, again with the chapter tiles selected

In the "Find what" box, type a hyphen with a space either side, that is " - " (without the quotation marks)

 In the "Replace with" box, type "^l" (this is the control code for a manual line break)

This changes all the occurrences in the selected text. Click No to skip the remainder of the document, to avoid changing hyphens elsewhere in the text

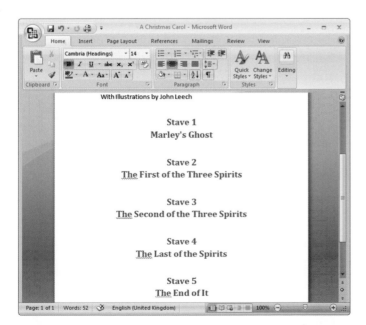

Don't forget

To see the line-break codes, click the Show/Hide button (in the Paragraph group on the Home tab). Note that each title remains a single item, even though spread over two lines.

Stave·1↵
Marley's·Ghost¶

Import Text

1 Click just to the right of the Stave 1 title and select Insert, Page Break to start the chapter on a new page

Hot tip

Type paragraphs of text, insert text from a file, or copy and paste text from a file, if you just want part of the contents.

2 Click the page, just past the end of the title, and press Enter, to add a new blank line (in Body Text style)

3 Select Insert, click Insert Object and choose Text from File

Don't forget

This option was known as Insert File in previous versions of Word. It allows you to transfer the contents from various file types, including Word, web and text.

4 Locate the file holding the required text and click Insert

5 Click OK to select the appropriate encoding, if prompted

Step 5 is required only when the system needs your help in interpreting the imported text.

The text will be copied to the document at the required location.

Repeat steps 1 to 5 for each chapter, to insert all the text for the book.

6 Click anywhere in the new text, click the Home tab, then click Select, and choose Select Text with Similar Formatting

7 Select your preferred style, e.g. Normal, No Spacing

The inserted text may not have the format you require, but you can change all the inserted text in a single operation.

8 All the text inserted into the document will be converted to the selected style

Insert Illustrations

1 Find the location for an illustration: for example, select Home, click Find and search for the appropriate text, such as "Figure: "

Hot tip

The text contains the titles for the illustration at the required locations, in the form: "Figure: Title of Illustration".

2 For each location, select the Insert tab and click Picture

Don't forget

You can insert pictures from image files of all the usual types, including bitmap, jpeg (photos) and gif (web graphics).

3 Locate the file containing the required illustration and click Insert

4 The picture is inserted into the document, in line with the text, and you can adjust its position

Add Captions

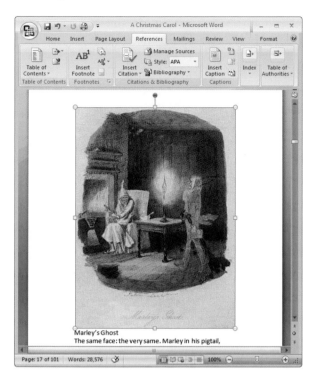

Don't forget

Repeat these steps to insert a picture and a caption for each of the illustrations in the book.

Don't forget

If the document doesn't already contain the title for the illustration, type it after the automatic number in the Caption box or directly into the document.

53

1 From the Reference tab, select Insert Caption and click OK

2 After the automatic number, type a colon ":" and insert the text for the picture title

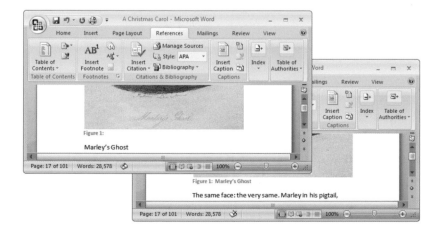

Hot tip

The captions that you add are used to create a table of illustrations (see page 56).

Table of Contents

When you have formatted text within the document with heading levels you can use these to create and maintain a contents list.

 Click the Page Number button on the Status bar, type "2" and click Go To, then Close, to move to that page

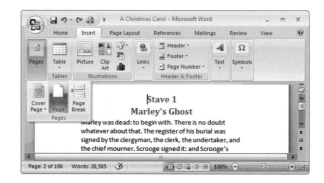

Don't forget

You could also select Insert, Page Break, to provide a new blank page ahead of the typing-cursor location.

 Select the Insert tab and click Blank Page in the Pages group, to insert a blank page for the contents list

Beware

Move to the new page (press the back arrow, or use the Go To command) to go to the new page 2, before selecting the Table of Contents button.

 On the References tab, click the Table of Contents button

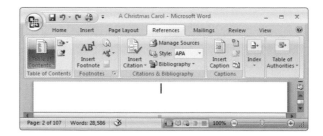

...cont'd

4 Choose the type of table that you want, for example Automatic Table 1 (with "Contents" as the title)

Hot tip

This type of table will use heading levels 1, 2 and 3 to generate the table. You can also build a table using custom styles, or based on manually selected text.

5 The table of contents is inserted. When it is selected, you can see that it is built up from field codes

Beware

The table of contents must be updated to show any changes to the heading-text content or the page-number value.

Don't forget

When you hover the mouse pointer over an entry in the table, with the shift key pressed, you'll have a link to the associated section of the document.

Table of Illustrations

 Go to the start of chapter 1 and insert another blank page, this time for a list of illustrations

 On the new page, type "Illustrations", select the Home tab, the arrow to expand the Styles group, and Heading 2

 Press Enter to add a blank line, then on the References tab click Insert Table of Figures

 Clear the box "Include label and number" if desired

Click OK to insert the table of figures

...cont'd

6 The table of figures is similar to the table of contents

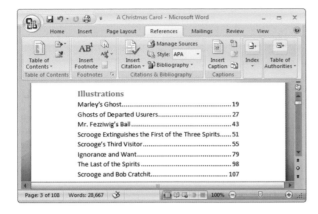

Don't forget

There's no heading included, so any heading required must be provided separately, in this case "Illustrations".

7 Click the table to see field codes and links to the figures

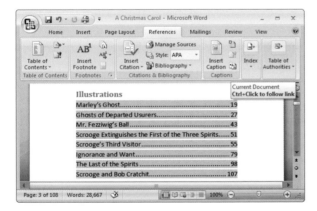

Hot tip

Text that is grayed when selected indicates that there is an underlying field code (a system value).

8 Highlight the whole table and select Toggle Field Codes

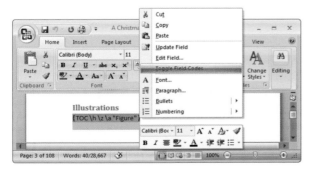

Don't forget

The format of the field code for the table of figures indicates that it is actually a TOC (table of contents) based on the "Figure" label.

Insert Preface

1 Go to page 2 (the contents page) and insert a blank page for the book preface

2 On the new page, type "Preface", select the Home tab, the arrow to expand the Styles group, and Heading 2

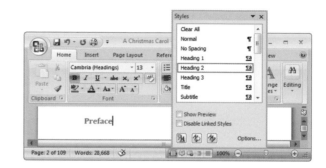

3 Press Enter and insert text from a file (see page 50) or type the text for the preface

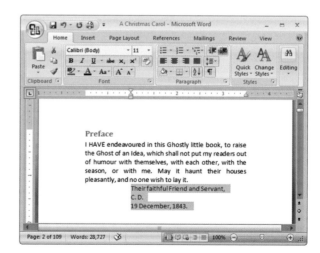

4 Adjust the formatting and alignment of the text as desired, for example selecting Justify for the main portion and Increase Indent for the signature section

5 Select Save on the Quick Access toolbar

Update Table of Contents

When you make changes, such as the preface or the illustrations list, that include new headings (level 1, 2 or 3), the table of contents is affected. However, the updates will not be displayed immediately. To apply the updates:

1 Locate the table of contents and click anywhere within it

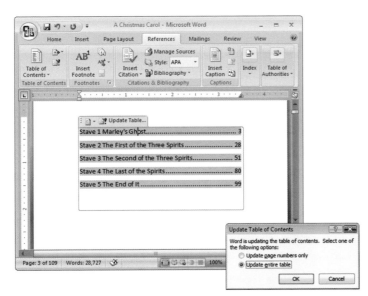

2 Select "Update entire table" and click OK

3 The new entries will be inserted, and the page numbers will be updated as appropriate

Hot tip

Whenever you add text to the document, or insert pages, the page numbers for the entries in the table of contents change, but the changes will not appear until you explicitly select Update Table.

Don't forget

If you've added pages or text to your document, but not changed the headings, select "Update page numbers only".

Decorate the Page

1 Select sections of text and choose the appropriate format

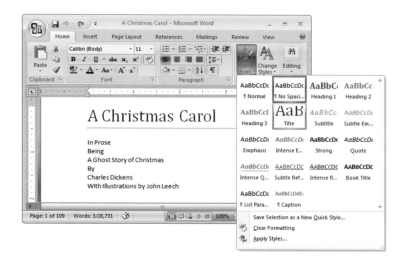

Hot tip

Finally, you can enhance the formatting of the title page, using styles or WordArt.

2 For example, select the book title and choose the Title style. There are also Subtitle and various Emphasis styles

Title style

Subtitle style

Intense Emphasis

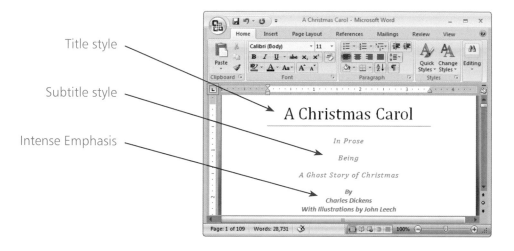

3 For more impact, select the item of text and from the Insert tab choose the WordArt option in the text group

1 Pick the style of WordArt to try (you can change it later)

Experiment with the styles and options provided for WordArt, to find the appearance that best suits the text you are working with.

2 Choose the font, for example Old English, set the size and attributes and edit the text if desired

3 The text is inserted using the WordArt style selected

Don't forget

Use the commands and buttons on the WordArt Format tab to edit the text, select a different style or change the fill, surround and shadow colors. You can also click and drag the handles to resize the WordArt text.

Templates

 Click the Office button, select New, and choose "New from existing", or select an installed template

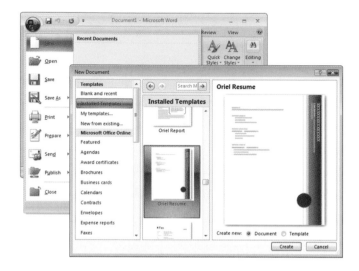

 For a new requirement, select the relevant Office Online category (and subcategory if offered); use the thumbnail and preview images to choose the most suitable template

...cont'd

3 Click the Download button for the required template. Your Office software is validated before the transfer starts

4 When the transfer completes, a new document is opened using the chosen template

5 Change the contents of the text boxes to personalize the document

6 In future you can select New, My Templates to use the template to create another document of that type

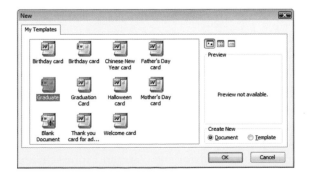

Don't forget

Each time you download from the Office Online website, your Office software is automatically checked. Click the box to hide the message for future downloads.

Don't forget

A two-fold document such as this greetings card will have part of the contents inserted upside down, so that it appears correctly after printing and folding.

Hot tip

When you download a template, it is added to My Templates (and to Recent Templates) so that you won't have to download it the next time it's needed.

Publisher

1 Start the Publisher application, if included in your edition of Office, to see the range of publication types supported

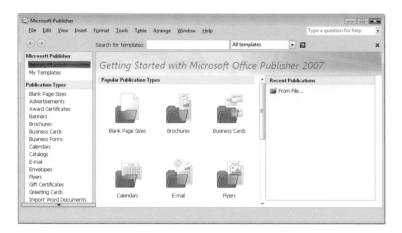

Publisher provides a higher level of desktop publishing capability, with a great variety of paper sizes and styles, many templates for brochures and leaflets etc., and lots of guidance.

2 For example, select the Greeting Cards category, and click the Congratulations card type

3 Click any template in the group to see an enlarged version and details of the color and font schemes

Don't forget

Publisher uses the menu and toolbar structure used in previous versions of Office, rather than the new Ribbon technology.

Microsoft Office
Publisher 2007

Hot tip

You can prepare your text in Word, which has superior text-entry capabilities, then import the Word documents into Publisher to create the final publication.

Don't forget

Customize the template before you use it to create your document, or make the changes later, in the document itself.

Create a Publication

1 Choose the template you want to use, for example Congratulations 2, and click the Create button

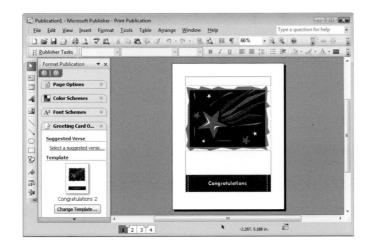

The greeting card is divided into four sections, each one-quarter of the physical page, to make it easier to view and edit individual parts of the card.

2 Click the link "Select a suggested verse", to review examples of sample text, then click OK to choose one

3 Click section 2 or 3 to see the middle portion of the card

You can make changes to the example you want to use, before or after you click OK.

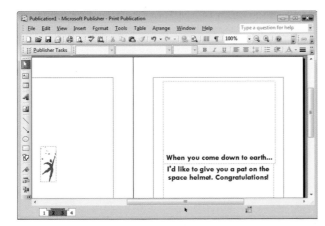

Print the Publication

1 Click section 4 to see the back portion of the card

Publisher presents the card in a professional form, complete with the publisher attribution. You can edit this text before printing the document.

Hot tip

Select File, Print to send the document to the printer (or press Ctrl+P).

2 Select File, Print Preview, to see how it will appear on paper

3 The document is shown as a single full page, with sections 2 and 3 inverted

Don't forget

Once printed, the page is folded in half horizontally, then in half again, to form the greeting card.

(4) Calculations

This looks at Excel, the spreadsheet application, and covers creating a new workbook, entering data, replicating values, formatting numbers, adding formulas and functions and using templates.

Start Excel

To start Microsoft Excel with a fresh new spreadsheet:

1 Click Start, All Programs, Microsoft Office and select Microsoft Office Excel 2007 to open with Book1

Hot tip

The file type will be .xlsx, indicating that it uses the new Office 2007 XML-based file format.

2 Alternatively, right-click an empty part of a folder window; select New, Microsoft Office Excel Worksheet

Beware

The New option only appears when you right-click an empty space between the existing file icons in the folder.

Don't forget

You can over-type the suggested file name to provide a more suitable name for your new worksheet.

 3 Double-click the file icon New Microsoft Office Excel Worksheet to display and edit the document

...cont'd

The spreadsheet presented is an Excel workbook that contains, initially, three worksheets, each of which is blank. The cells that it contains are empty – all 17 million of them.

Hot tip

There can be up to 1048576 rows and 16384 columns. This compares with 65536 rows and 256 columns in previous releases.

1. To move to the last row (1048576) in the worksheet, press End and then press the down arrow

2. To move to the last column (XFD) in the worksheet, press End and then press the right arrow

If the worksheet contains data, the action taken depends on the initial location.

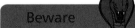

Beware

It may be impractical to utilize even a fraction of the total number of cells available, but the enlarged sheet size does give greater flexibility in designing spreadsheets.

3. If the selected cell contains data, pressing End and then an arrow key takes you to the edge of the data area

4. If the current cell is empty, you move to the start of the adjacent data area

5. If there's no more data in that direction, you'll move to the edge of the worksheet, as with an empty worksheet

Don't forget

The movement is always in the direction of the arrow key selected.

Enter Data

The most common use of spreadsheets is for financial planning, for example to keep track of income and expenditure. To create a family budget:

 Open a blank worksheet, select cell A1 and type the title for the spreadsheet, e.g. "Family Budget"

 Press the Enter or down key to insert the text and move to cell A2, and type the next entry, "Income"

Repeat this process to add the remaining labels for the income and expense items you want to track

...cont'd

If you omit an item, you can insert an additional worksheet row. For example, to include a second "Salary" income item:

 1 Click a cell (e.g. C4) in the row that's just below where the new entry is required and select Insert, Insert Sheet Rows from the Cells group on the Home tab

2 Enter the additional label, e.g. "Salary 2nd", in A4

3 Double-click an existing cell to edit or retype the entry, for example to change "Salary" to "Salary 1st" in A3

Quick Fill

You can create one column of data, then let Excel replicate the cell contents for you. For example:

 Enter monthly values in column C, for example "January" in C2 and values in cells C3–C7 and C10–C15

72

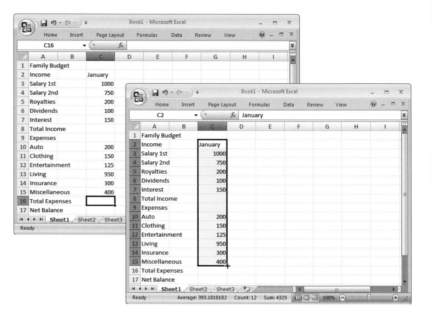

2 Highlight cells C2–C15, move the mouse pointer over the box at the bottom right, and when it becomes **+** then drag to the right to replicate the cells for further months

...cont'd

3 Release the mouse pointer when the required number of columns is indicated

Don't forget

Having initialized the cells, you can edit or replace the contents of any cells to complete the information needed.

4 Numeric values are duplicated, but the month name is detected, and the succeeding months are inserted

After you've used the Fill handle, the Auto Fill Options button appears. Click this to control the action, for example to replicate the formatting only, or to copy cells without devising a series.

Hot tip

Excel detects weekdays to create a series such as Monday, Tuesday ...; and it detects abbreviated names such as Jan, Feb ... or Mon, Tue ....

5 When you've entered data into the worksheet, remember to periodically click the Save button on the Quick Access toolbar to store the file

Don't forget

The first time you click the Save button, you'll be prompted to provide a file name in place of the default Book1.

73

Sums and Differences

When you've entered the data and made the changes required, you can introduce functions and formulas to complete the worksheet.

 1 Click cell C8 (total income for January), then select the Home tab and click the Sum button

	A	B	C	D	E	F	G	H	I
1	Family Budget								
2	Income		January	February	March	April	May	June	
3	Salary 1st		1000	1000	1000	1000	1000	1000	
4	Salary 2nd		750	750	750	750	750	750	
5	Royalties		500	300	100	50	0	500	
6	Dividends		100	100	100	150	150	150	
7	Interest		150	150	150	150	150	150	
8	Total Income		=SUM(C3:C7)						

Don't forget

The numerical cells in a block immediately adjacent to the selected cell will be selected and included in the Sum function. Always check that Excel has selected the appropriate cells.

2 Press Enter to show the total, then repeat the procedure for cell C16 (total expenses for January)

	A	B	C	D	E	F	G	H	I
2	Income		January	February	March	April	May	June	
3	Salary 1st		1000	1000	1000	1000	1000	1000	
4	Salary 2nd		750	750	750	750	750	750	
5	Royalties		500	300	100	50	0	500	
6	Dividends		100	100	100	150	150	150	
7	Interest		150	150	150	150	150	150	
8	Total Income		2500						
9	Expenses								
10	Auto		200	200	200	200	200	200	
11	Clothing		150	150	150	150	150	150	
12	Entertainment		125	150	175	125	50	125	
13	Living		950	950	950	950	950	950	
14	Insurance		300	300	300	300	300	300	
15	Miscellaneous		400	400	400	400	400	400	
16	Total Expenses		2125						
17	Net Balance								

3 Click in cell C17 (net balance for January)

4 Type "=", click C8, type "-", click C16 (to calculate total income for January minus total expenses for January)

Hot tip

The = symbol indicates that the following text is a formula. You can type the cell references, or click on the cell itself and Excel will enter the appropriate reference.

	A	B	C	D	E	F	G	H	I
7	Interest		150	150	150	150	150	150	
8	Total Income		2500						
9	Expenses								
10	Auto		200	200	200	200	200	200	
11	Clothing		150	150	150	150	150	150	
12	Entertainment		125	150	175	125	50	125	
13	Living		950	950	950	950	950	950	
14	Insurance		300	300	300	300	300	300	
15	Miscellaneous		400	400	400	400	400	400	
16	Total Expenses		2125						
17	Net Balance		=C8-C16						

(Formula bar: SUM, =C8-C16)

5 Press Enter to complete the formula and display the result

6 Select cell C8 and use the Fill handle to replicate the formula for the other months (e.g. February to June), and repeat this process for cells C16 and C17

(Formula bar: C17, =C8-C16)

	A	B	C	D	E	F	G	H	I
1	Family Budget								
2	Income		January	February	March	April	May	June	
3	Salary 1st		1000	1000	1000	1000	1000	1000	
4	Salary 2nd		750	750	750	750	750	750	
5	Royalties		500	300	100	50	0	500	
6	Dividends		100	100	100	150	150	150	
7	Interest		150	150	150	150	150	150	
8	Total Income		2500	2300	2100	2100	2050	2550	
9	Expenses								
10	Auto		200	200	200	200	200	200	
11	Clothing		150	150	150	150	150	150	
12	Entertainment		125	150	175	125	50	125	
13	Living		950	950	950	950	950	950	
14	Insurance		300	300	300	300	300	300	
15	Miscellaneous		400	400	400	400	400	400	
16	Total Expenses		2125	2150	2175	2125	2050	2125	
17	Net Balance		375	150	-75	-25	0	425	

(Status bar: Ready, Average: 141.6666667, Count: 6, Sum: 850, 100%)

Don't forget

When the formula is replicated, the cell references, e.g. C8:C16, are incremented, to D8:D16, E8:E16 etc.

Formatting

Hot tip

Changing the format for various parts of the worksheet can make it easier to review and assess the results.

1 Click A1 (the title cell), then select the Home tab, choose a larger font size, and select a font effect such as Bold

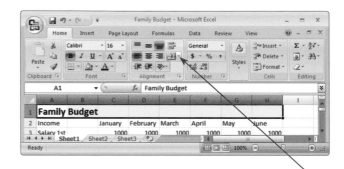

2 Press Shift and click H1 to highlight the row across the data, then click the Merge and Center button

	A	B	C	D	E	F	G	H	I
1				**Family Budget**					
2	**Income**		January	February	March	April	May	June	
3	Salary 1st		1000	1000	1000	1000	1000	1000	
4	Salary 2nd		750	750	750	750	750	750	
5	Royalties		500	300	100	50	0	500	
6	Dividends		100	100	100	150	150	150	
7	Interest		150	150	150	150	150	150	
8	**Total Income**		2500	2300	2100	2100	2050	2550	
9	**Expenses**								
10	Auto		200	200	200	200	200	200	
11	Clothing		150	150	150	150	150	150	
12	Entertainment		125	150	175	125	50	125	
13	Living		950	950	950	950	950	950	
14	Insurance		300	300	300	300	300	300	
15	Miscellaneous		400	400	400	400	400	400	
16	**Total Expenses**		2125	2150	2175	2125	2050	2125	
17	**Net Balance**		375	150	-75	-25	0	425	

Don't forget

You can change each cell individually, or press Ctrl, click each of the cells to select them, and then apply the changes to all the cells at once.

3 Click the Categories and Totals labels (e.g. A2, A8, A9, A16, A17) and change the font size and effects

4 Alternatively, click Styles to pick a suitable cell style

...cont'd

To emphasize the "Net Balance" values for each month:

1 Select the range of cells, e.g. C17:H17

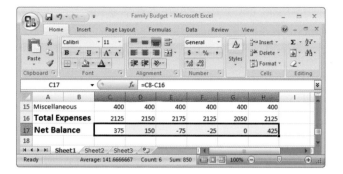

Hot tip

Excel 2007 includes a very useful Conditional Formatting facility, where the effects applied depend on the actual contents of the cells being formatted.

2 Select Styles, Conditional Formatting, Color Scales and choose for example the Green–Yellow–Red color scale

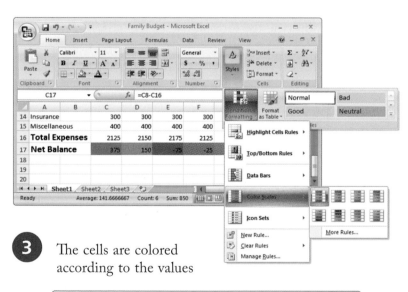

3 The cells are colored according to the values

Don't forget

Positive balances are green; the larger the balance, the deeper the shade; modest balances are yellow; while shades of red are applied to negative balances.

Rounding Up

You can use Excel to help you solve numerical problems, such as the number of tiles needed to cover the floor area of a room.

1 Open a new, blank worksheet and enter these labels in the first column:
Number of Tiles
Tile Length
Tile Width
Room Length
Room Width
Number
Per Box
Boxes

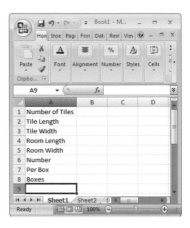

2 Enter sample sizes in cells B2:B5, making sure that you use the same units for the tile and the room dimensions

3 In cell B6 type the formula "=(B4/B2)*(B5/B3)"

4 In cell B8 type the formula "=B6/B7"

However, if you try to fit the tiles to the area, you'll find that some tiles have to be cut. The wastage leaves part of the area uncovered.

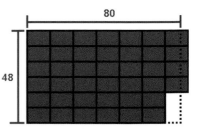

...cont'd

To ensure that there are enough whole tiles to completely cover the area, you need to round up the evaluations:

 1 Copy B2:B8 to C2:C8, and in cell C6 type the formula "=CEILING(B4/B2,1)*CEILING(B5/B3,1)"

Hot tip

The CEILING function rounds the results up to the next significant value, in this case the next highest integer. If the tiles have a repeat pattern, you might need to use the pattern size as the significant number.

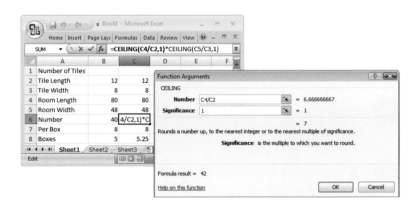

The number of whole tiles increases to 42, which will now cover the complete floor area, even after cutting.

This gives 5.25 boxes. Assuming that boxes must be purchased in whole numbers, this result also needs rounding up.

 2 Copy C2:C8 to D2:D8, and in cell D8 type the formula "=ROUNDUP(D6/D7,0)" to get the result: 6 boxes

Don't forget

This rounds up the result to zero decimal places, which gives the next highest integer.

Find a Function

There are a large number of functions available in Excel, so they are organized into a library of groups to make it easier to find the one you need.

1 Select the Formulas tab to show the Function Library

2 Click a category in the Function Library for an alphabetic list of functions it offers

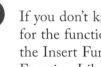

3 If you don't know where to search for the function you want, click the Insert Function button in the Function Library

4 Choose a category and pick a function from the list

5 Alternatively, type a description and click Go, then select one of the recommended functions

6 Select a suitable function, e.g. PMT, and click OK

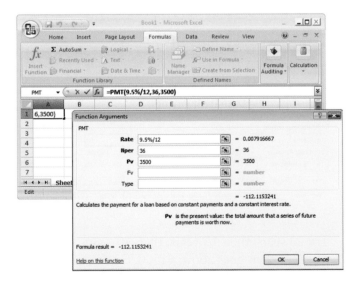

Don't forget

Rate is the interest rate for the payment interval (e.g. per month), Nper is the number of periods (e.g. number of months) and Pv is the present value (loan amount).

7 Type the values for the arguments (Rate, Nper, etc.) using the description provided as you select each item

Hot tip

You can optionally provide a final value Fv (the cash balance), and also specify the Type (payments made at the start or the end of each period).

8 The result is displayed (a negative figure, indicating a payment) and the function is inserted into the worksheet

Goal Seeking

Using the PMT function, you can establish the monthly payments required to pay off a long-term loan over, say, 25 years.

Suppose, however, you'd like to know how many years it will take to pay off the loan, if you increase the payments to, say, $1500.

1   One way to establish this is by trial and error, adjusting the number of years until you get the required payment

2   Try 20 years, then 15 years, then 10 years, and the payment then goes above $1500. So the appropriate period would be between 10 and 15 years

However, Excel provides an automatic way to apply this type of process, and this can give you an exact answer very quickly.

...cont'd

1 Click the cell containing the function, select the Data tab and click the What If Analysis button in Data Tools

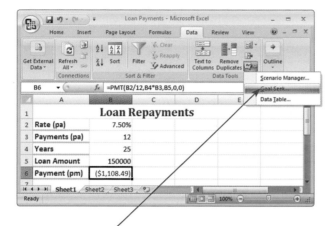

Hot tip

Use the Scenario Manager to create a set of results for a range of values, such as 10, 15 and 20 years of repayments.

2 Select the Goal Seek option and specify the required result –1500 (payment per month) and the changing cell B4 (number of years)

3 Goal Seeking tries out various values for the changing cell, until the desired solution is found

Beware

You must specify the target payment as a negative value since it is a repayment, otherwise Goal Seeking will be unable to find a solution.

4 Click OK to return to the worksheet with its revised results

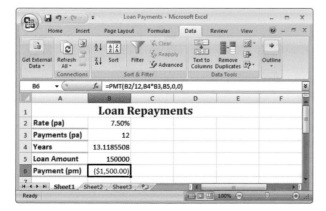

Templates

 Select the Office button and click the New button

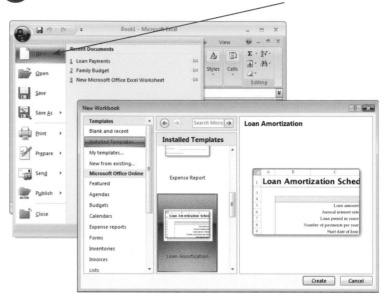

 Select Installed Templates or "My Templates" to choose from the list of templates already on your system

Select a category to review the templates on Microsoft Office Online, and click Download to install

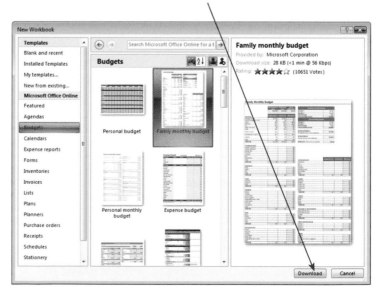

5 Manage Data

Excel also manages data, so we look at importing data, applying sorts and filters, and selecting specific sets of data. The data can be used to create a chart, or you can arrange the data in tables, insert totals and computations and look up values. For more advanced requirements, some editions of Office include Access, which offers full database management functions.

Import Data

You don't always need to type in all the information in your worksheets, if the data is already available in another application. For example, to import data from a delimited text file:

Hot tip

Excel can retrieve data from database systems including SQL Server, Access, dBase, FoxPro, Oracle and Paradox, or from any application that can create files in a delimited text file format such as CSV (comma-separated values).

1 Click the Office button and select Open

Don't forget

Identify the appropriate file type to select from, in this case, Text Files.

2 Select the file that contains the data you wish to import and click Open to start the Text Import Wizard, which recognizes the delimited file. Click Next to continue

3 Choose the delimiter (e.g. Comma) and click Next

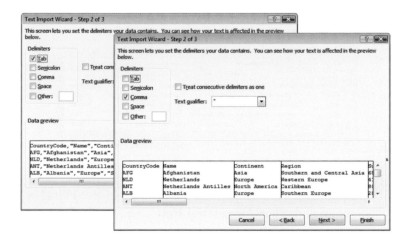

Hot tip

When you choose a delimiter, you can see the effect on the text in the preview area.

Don't forget

The default format is General, which will handle most situations, but you can select specific data formats where appropriate.

4 Adjust column formats if required, then click Finish

5 The data is presented in the form of an Excel worksheet

Explore the Data

Don't forget

Select the Office button, click Save As and choose file type Excel Workbook to save the data as a standard Excel file.

1 Double-click or drag the separators between columns to reveal more of the data that they contain

2 Select the View tab, click Freeze Panes in the Window group and select Freeze Top Row

Hot tip

Freezing the top row makes the headings that it contains visible, whichever part of the worksheet is being displayed.

3 Press Ctrl+End to move to the last cell in the data area

Hot tip

This will show you how many rows and columns there are in the data (in this example, 240 rows and 13 columns).

Sort

1 Click a cell in the "Name" column, select the Data tab and click the A–Z (ascending) button to sort by name

You can also select the Sort options from within the Editing group on the Home tab.

2 Click a cell in the "Population" column and click the Z–A (sort descending) button, to sort from highest to lowest

Excel automatically selects all the surrounding data and sorts whole rows into the required order.

You can sort the data into sequence using several levels of values.

3 To sort by more than one value, click the Sort button

...cont'd

Beware

If a selection of the worksheet is highlighted when you click one of the buttons, the sort may be restricted to the selected data.

Don't forget

For data organized by columns rather than rows, click the Options button and select "Sort left to right".

4 Click the arrow in the "Sort by" box and select the main sort value, for example "Continent"

5 Click the Add Level button and select the additional sort values, for example "Region" and then "Population"

6 Change the sort sequence if needed, then click OK to sort the data by population within region and continent

	A	B	C	D	E	F	G
1	CountryCode	Name	Continent	Region	SurfaceArea	Indep	Population
192	PAN	Panama	North America	Central America	75517	1903	2856000
193	BLZ	Belize	North America	Central America	22696	1981	241000
194	USA	United States	North America	North America	9363520	1776	278357000
195	CAN	Canada	North America	North America	9970610	1867	31147000
196	BMU	Bermuda	North America	North America	53		65000
197	GRL	Greenland	North America	North America	2166090		56000
198	SPM	Saint Pierre and Miqu	North America	North America	242		7000
199	AUS	Australia	Oceania	Australia and New Zealand	7741220	1901	18886000
200	NZL	New Zealand	Oceania	Australia and New Zealand	270534	1907	3862000
201	CXR	Christmas Island	Oceania	Australia and New Zealand	135		2500
202	NFK	Norfolk Island	Oceania	Australia and New Zealand	36		2000
203	CCK	Cocos (Keeling) Island	Oceania	Australia and New Zealand	14		600
204	PNG	Papua New Guinea	Oceania	Melanesia	462840	1975	4807000
205	FJI	Fiji Islands	Oceania	Melanesia	18274	1970	817000

Filters

You can filter the data to hide the entries that are not of immediate interest.

 1 Click a cell within the data area, select the Data tab and click the Filter button in the Sort & Filter group

Hot tip

You can also select the Filter button from within the Editing group on the Home tab (see page 89).

2 Click a filter icon, e.g. on Continent, to display its AutoFilter

3 Click the Select All box, to deselect all entries, then select the specific entry you want, e.g. Oceania

4 Click OK to apply the filter

Hot tip

Filtering is turned on, and a filter icon (an arrow) is added to each heading, with an initial setting of Showing All.

91

Number Filters

You can set number filters, where you specify a level at which to accept or reject entries, or choose an option such as accepting the top ten entries.

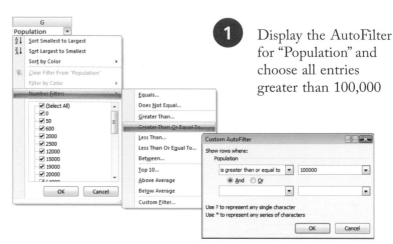

1 Display the AutoFilter for "Population" and choose all entries greater than 100,000

2 The filter icons for modified AutoFilters are changed to show that filtering is in effect for those particular columns

If you click the Filter button on the Data tab or the Home tab, it will remove all the filters and delete all the filter settings.

3 Click a filter icon and select the Clear Filter option to remove the filter for a particular column

4 The filter icon for that column reverts to an arrow, and the Showing All option will be applied

Select Specific Data

Suppose you want to examine the population values for the larger countries. You can hide away the information that's not relevant for that purpose:

1 Use the AutoFilter on the "Population" column to display only countries whose populations are greater than 150 million

2 Click column A, press Ctrl, click columns C, D etc. and select Home, Format, Hide & Unhide, Hide Columns

3 The display will be restricted to the required data

This places the country names adjacent to the surface area and population values, ready for further analysis.

Hot tip

Filter the rows and hide selected columns to remove from view the data not needed at the moment.

Don't forget

Sort the information if required, for example in descending order of population size.

Create a Chart

1 Highlight the data (including headers), then select the Insert tab and click the arrow on the Charts group

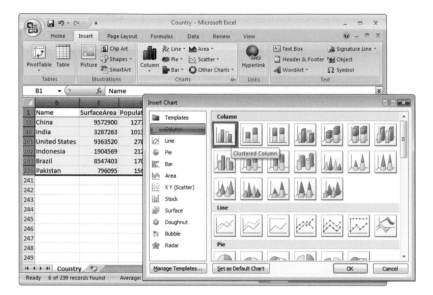

2 Choose the chart type and subtype, in this case Column and Clustered Column

3 Click one of the "Population" columns and select Format Data Series

Format Data Series

Series Options

Fill
Border Color
Border Styles
Shadow
3-D Format

Series Options

Series Overlap
Separated ———○——— Overlapped
0%

Gap Width
No Gap ——○———— Large Gap
150%

Plot Series On
● Primary Axis
○ Secondary Axis

Close

Format Data Series

Series Options

Fill
Border Color
Border Styles
Shadow
3-D Format

Series Options

Series Overlap
Separated ———○——— Overlapped
0%

Gap Width
No Gap ————○— Large Gap
400%

Plot Series On
○ Primary Axis
● Secondary Axis

Close

By default, one data series would overlay the other, but adjusting the width for one of them allows you to view both sets of data together.

4 Choose Plot Series On Secondary Axis, and adjust Gap Width to 400%

5 Use the Format tab to provide titles for the chart and the axes and to adjust the position of the legend

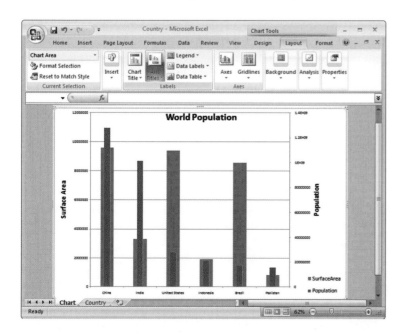

Select the Move Chart button on the Design tab to place the chart on a separate worksheet.

Import a List

The "Country" worksheet discussed previously includes the "Capital" column, which provides a link to a list of cities. If this list is available as a text file, you can import it into the worksheet.

 1 Select a cell marking the start of an empty section of the worksheet, and select the Data tab

 2 Click Get External Data and choose From Text

 3 Locate the text file and select Import, then follow the steps of the Text Import Wizard (see page 86)

 4 Click OK to place the data in the current worksheet, at the location selected initially

Create a Table

1 Click a cell within the data range and select the Insert tab, then click the Table button

2 Click Yes to confirm the range and accept the headers

3 The table will be created (using the default style)

Add Totals to Table

Hot tip

Convert the range of country data into table form, then add totals.

Don't forget

The functions that you choose are entered as subfunctions of Subset, for example:

101	Average
102	Count numbers
103	Count
104	Max
105	Min
109	Sum

1 Click a cell within the country data, and select Insert, Table, then rename the new table as "Country"

2 Select the Table Tools Design tab, click the box for Total Row, then scroll to the bottom (press End then down)

3 Select the Total box for "Name", click the arrow and choose the function, e.g. Count

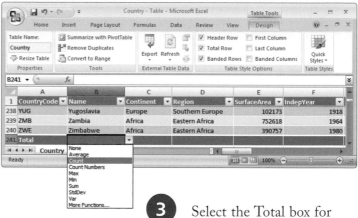

4 Select the Sum function for columns with numerical values, such as "SurfaceArea", "Population" or "GNP"

	A	B	C	D	E	F
E241	fx	=SUBTOTAL(109,[SurfaceArea])				
1	CountryCode	Name	Continent	Region	SurfaceArea	IndepYear
238	YUG	Yugoslavia	Europe	Southern Europe	102173	1918
239	ZMB	Zambia	Africa	Eastern Africa	752618	1964
240	ZWE	Zimbabwe	Africa	Eastern Africa	390757	1980
241	Total		239		148956306.9	

Hot tip

You do not use the column and row labels to specify cells and ranges, you use the header name for the column (enclosed in square brackets).

5 You can combine functions such as Min and Max, to show the range of values contained in a column such as "IndepYear"

	A	B	C	D	E	F
F241	fx	=CONCATENATE("From ",SUBTOTAL(105,[IndepYear])," to ",SUBTOTAL(104,[IndepYear]))				
1	CountryCode	Name	Continent	Region	SurfaceArea	IndepYear
238	YUG	Yugoslavia	Europe	Southern Europe	102173	1918
239	ZMB	Zambia	Africa	Eastern Africa	752618	1964
240	ZWE	Zimbabwe	Africa	Eastern Africa	390757	1980
241	Total		239		148956306.9	From -1523 to 1994

Don't forget

The headers contain AutoFilter icons, so you can limit the display to a section of the table.

6 When a column contains a set of discrete values, such as "Continent" or "Region", you can calculate the number of unique values that it contains

	A	B	C	D	E	F
C241	fx	{=SUM(1/COUNTIF([Continent],[Continent]))}				
1	CountryCode	Name	Continent	Region	SurfaceArea	IndepYear
238	YUG	Yugoslavia	Europe	Southern Europe	102173	1918
239	ZMB	Zambia	Africa	Eastern Africa	752618	1964
240	ZWE	Zimbabwe	Africa	Eastern Africa	390757	1980
241	Total		239	7	25	148956306.9 From -1523 to 1994

Don't forget

You can use any Excel function in the total boxes, not just the Subtotal function.

This counts the number of times each individual value in the column is repeated, and uses these repeats to build up a count of the number of distinct values.

Computed Column

You can insert a column in the table without affecting other ranges or data or tables in the worksheet.

1 Click in the "Population" column, select the Home tab, click Insert, and choose Insert Table Columns to the Left

2 The new column is inserted and initially named Column1

3 Type a new name, such as "Density", and press Enter

Click in the first cell of the column, and type "=", then click the "Population" cell in the same row

 Type "/", then click the "SurfaceArea" cell in the same row

101

Press Enter, and the expression is evaluated and copied to all the other cells in the table column

Table Lookup

The "Country" table contains a city code number for the capital city of each country, rather than the actual name.

The names are stored in the separate "City" table, which has details of more than 4000 cities.

To display the name of the capital city alongside the city number in the "Country" table:

1 Insert a table column next to the "Capital" column, and change its name to "CapitalCity"

2 In the first cell of this column type the expression "=VLOOKUP("

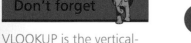

3 Click the adjacent cell in the "Capital" column, then type ",City,2,0)"

4 Press Enter, and the capital-city name is inserted, on all the rows in the "Country" table, not just the current row

5 Scroll down to check the entries for particular countries, for example the United States (Washington) or the United Kingdom (London)

Manage Data Using Access

You'll find Access 2007 in the Professional, Enterprise or Ultimate editions of Office 2007.

Microsoft Office Access 2007

If you have large amounts of data or complex functions to handle, you may require the more comprehensive facilities in Access 2007.

1 Start Access from the Office folder on the Start menu and you'll be greeted by a range of database templates

Access uses the Office 2007 Fluent user interface (Ribbon technology), and can share data with other Office applications such as Excel, Word and PowerPoint.

2 Select a suitable template, for example Assets, change the suggested name if desired and click the Download button

3 Your copy of Office is validated, the selected template is downloaded and a new database is opened within Access

Access automatically displays a Help window, which offers advice on modifying and using your new database.

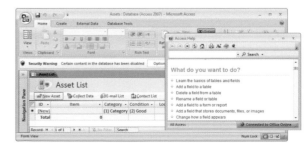

Security Within Access

1   Click the Options button on the Security Warning

2   This tells you that Access has disabled the VBA macros included in the template (the default security option)

3   Click "Enable this content" (for the current session only)

4   Click the Shutter Bar Open/Close button to display the list of database objects (tables and reports etc.)

Add Records

Hot tip

You can type directly into the cells of the asset table if you wish, rather than using the form.

1 Click the New Asset button to add an entry to the Assets database

📇 New Asset

2 Enter the details for the item, selecting from a list of values on fields with an arrow, e.g. Category

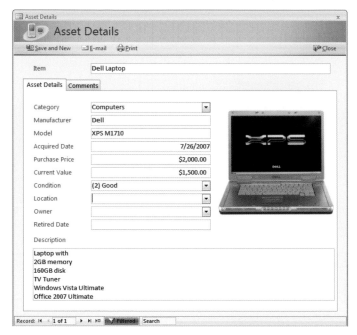

Hot tip

You can attach a link to a photograph of the asset if you wish.

Double-click to view or add attachments.

3 If the value you want is not listed, just right-click the box and select Edit List Items

✂	Cut
📋	Copy
📋	Paste
A↓	Sort A to Z
Z↓	Sort Z to A
✏	Edit List Items...

4 Add or change entries as required and click OK

Don't forget

The current record is automatically saved when you click Close, even if all the details are not completed.

Edit List Items

Type each item on a separate line:

Lounge
Family Room
Study
Bedroom
Utility Room
Kitchen
Hall
Workshop

Default Value:

OK   Cancel

5 Click Save and New to save the current record and begin the record for a new asset

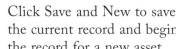

6 Presentations

Build a presentation, slide by slide, apply themes to create a consistent effect, and use animation to focus attention on particular points. Use a second monitor for a presenter view. Take advantage of templates, built in or downloaded, and print handouts for the presentation. Rehearse the show to get timings and create an automatic show.

Start a Presentation

Like Word, Excel and Access, the PowerPoint application uses the Office Fluent user interface (Ribbon technology), and displays tabs appropriate to the current activity.

To start PowerPoint and create a new presentation:

 1 Select Start, All Programs, Microsoft Office and click the PowerPoint entry

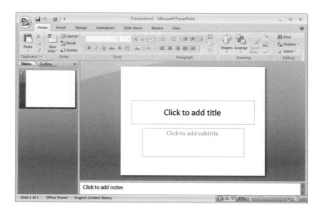

 2 Click to add a title as suggested, and type the title for the slide show, for example "Dickens World"

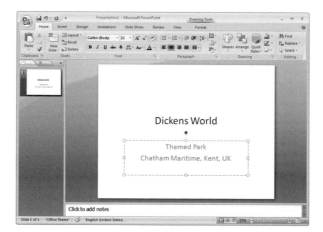

 3 Click to add a subtitle, the second option, and type, e.g. "Themed Park, Chatham Maritime, Kent, UK" (the childhood home of Charles Dickens)

...cont'd

4 Select the Home tab and click the New Slide button in the Slides group

5 An empty title and content slide is added to the slide show

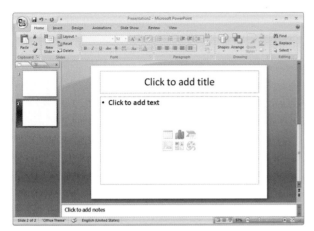

Hot tip

The new slide has option buttons to insert a table, chart, SmartArt graphic, picture from a file, clip art or media clip. See page 111 for an example.

6 Click on the prompts and add a title "Features of Dickens World" and bullet points to give the details

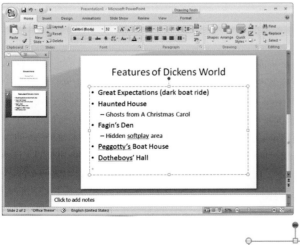

Don't forget

Click within a bullet item and press Shift+Tab to move it up (promote it) to the next level.

7 Press Enter to add a new bullet item, and the Tab key to move to the next lower level of bullet items

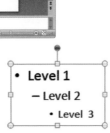

Expand the Slide

1 Continue to add items and you'll see the text size and spacing adjusted to fit the text onto the slide

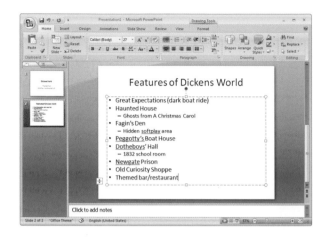

110

2 Click the AutoFit Options button and select the option to Split Text Between Two Slides

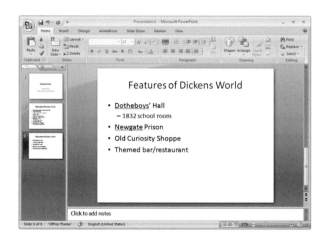

3 A new slide is inserted, with the same layout and title as the original slide, and the bullet items are shared evenly between the two slides

Insert a Picture

1 Select the Home tab and click the arrow on the New Slide button in the Slides group to display the options

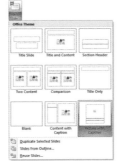

2 Choose a slide layout such as Picture with Caption

3 Click the icon to add a picture, as suggested in the prompt

Hot tip

There are nine standard layouts for slides, so you can select the one that's most appropriate for the specific content planned for each slide.

4 Locate and select the image file and click Insert, then "Click to add title", and "Click to add text"

Don't forget

The title and the text that you add provide the caption for the inserted image.

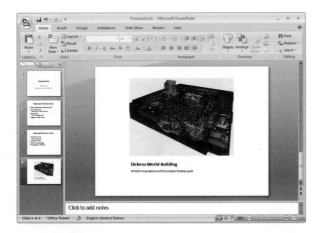

Apply a Theme

The default slides have a plain background, but you can choose a more effective theme and apply it to all the slides you've created.

1 Select the Design tab, and move the mouse pointer over each of the themes to see the effect

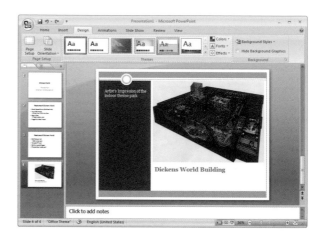

2 Click the preferred theme to apply it to all of the slides in the presentation

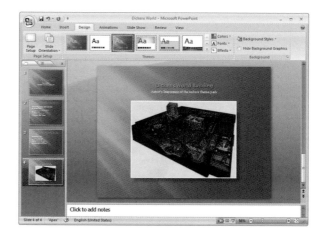

Apply to All Slides
Apply to Selected Slides
Set as Default Theme
Add Gallery to Quick Access Toolbar

3 You can scroll the list to display additional themes, change the colors, fonts and effects for the current theme, and modify the type of background style it uses

...cont'd

To select the transition effects between slides:

 Select the Animations tab and review the options – Wipes, Push and Cover, Stripes and Bars, Random

 Click the up and down arrows to view another row of effects, or click the More button to see the full list

 Click an effect to assign it to the current slide only, or click the button labelled Apply To All

By default, each slide advances to the next slide when you press the mouse key, but you can adjust the setting for individual slides.

 Clear the On Mouse Click box to disable the mouse-key option for the current slide

 Select the current slide to advance Automatically After a specified number of minutes and seconds

Whatever the setting, you can always advance the slide show by pressing one of the keyboard shortcuts, such as N (next), Enter, Page Down, right arrow or spacebar. To go back a step, you'd press P (previous), Page Up, left arrow, up arrow or Backspace.

Hot tip

Move the mouse pointer over an effect to see it demonstrated on the current slide, e.g. Wheel Clockwise, 8 Spokes.

Don't forget

You can choose a sound that will play between slides, and you can set the transition speed as slow, medium or fast.

Don't forget

If you have specified animation effects for individual elements on a slide (see page 114), the Advance function invokes the next animation rather than the next slide.

113

Animations

You can apply animation effects to individual parts of a slide.

Don't forget

The animation can be Fade, Wipe or Fly In, and may be applied All At Once or By 1st Level Paragraph.

 Select the Animations tab, pick a slide with bullet items and note that the Animate button is grayed (inactive)

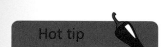

If you specify animation within the slide, you may want to enable automatic advance, unless you plan to manually display each line of the slide.

 Select the text box with the bullet items, and the Animate button is activated

 Click the down arrow on the Animate box and choose, for example, Fly In, By 1st Level Paragraph, then click the Preview button to observe the effect

Hot tip

Select Custom Animation to specify effects at entrance, for emphasis, and at exit, and to define the motion paths.

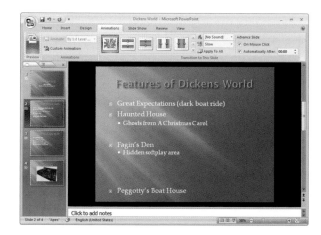

Run the Show

When you've added all the slides you need, you can try running the complete show to see the overall effect.

1 Select the Slide Show tab and click the From the Beginning button in the Start Slide Show group

2 The slides are displayed full-screen, with the transition and animation effects that you selected

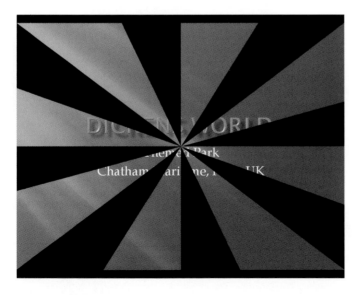

3 Click the final screen to terminate the slide show

You can also press F5 to run the slide show from the beginning, press Shift+F5 to run from the current slide, and press Esc to terminate.

Don't forget

You may need to use the mouse key or the keyboard shortcuts to go to the next slide or animation, if you haven't specified time limits for advancing slides.

Hot tip

When the slide show finishes, a black screen is presented, with the message: "End of slide show, click to exit."

Other Views

1 Select the View tab and select Slide Sorter to display all the slides so that you can rearrange their sequence

Hot tip

This view is very helpful when you have a larger number of slides, since you can simply drag slides into their new positions.

Don't forget

Each slide and its notes will be displayed on a single sheet, which can be printed to make a very useful handout.

2 Select the Notes Page view to see the current slide with its notes (information and prompts for the presenter)

Hot tip

There's also a Slide Show button provided in the Presentation Views group on the Views tab.

3 Click the Zoom button and select a zoom level to examine parts of the slide or the notes, then click OK

4 Select Fit and click OK, or click the Fit to Window button, to resize the view to make the whole page visible

5 You can also drag the slider on the zoom bar to change the size

...cont'd

6 To switch back to the view with slide bar and current slide, click the Normal button

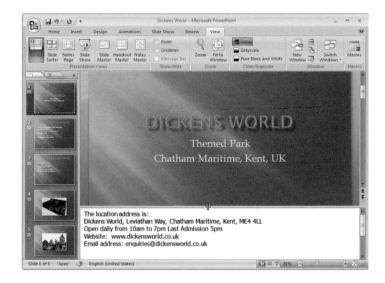

7 To reveal more of the notes area, click and drag the separator bar

8 Click the Outline tab to see the text contents of the slides, giving a summary view of the presentation, then click the Slides tab to redisplay the slides bar

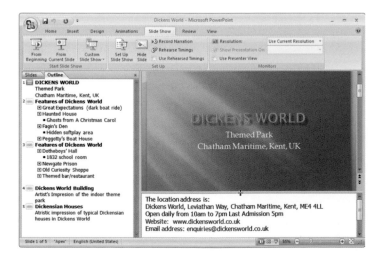

The view you select will be retained when you select another tab, so you should revert to the required view before leaving.

117

The buttons next to the Zoom bar provide the Normal, Slide Sorter and Slide Show views

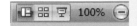

Presenter View

 1 Select the Slide Show tab and click the box to enable the Use Presenter View option

 2 If you do not have a second monitor enabled, you'll be warned that this a requirement for Presenter View

3 Click Check, and the Display Settings panel is opened

4 Select the second monitor and extend the desktop

 5 Click Yes to keep these settings

6 With dual-monitor support enabled, you will be able to select the Use Presenter View option

7 Select the View tab and click the Slide Show button to run the presentation on two monitors

You can also run the slide show from the Slide Show tab (see page 115).

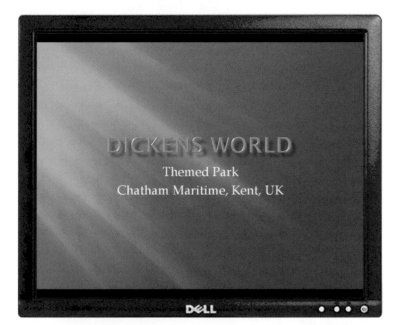

The first monitor displays the slide show in full-screen mode. The second monitor gives the presenter's view, with the current slide, its associated notes and the slide bar which will let you change the sequence in mid-flow.

Use the Zoom button to enlarge the notes and make them easier to read while giving the presentation.

Use a Template

Templates provide ready-built presentations, which can be adapted to your needs. They also offer examples of useful PowerPoint techniques.

120

 To review your templates, click the Office button, then click New and select a category, e.g. Installed Templates

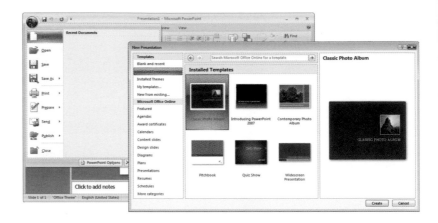

2 Select a template, for example Widescreen Presentation, and click the Create button to see the contents

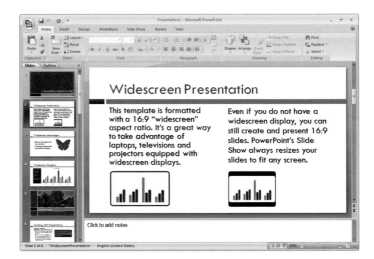

The templates that you open will be added to the Recently Used Templates list.

3 Select the View tab and click Slide Sorter to get an overview, or click Slide Show to see the presentation

 Presentations you create from templates will be saved only when you explicitly select the Save command

...cont'd

Open one of the Photo Album templates:

 1 Select the Office button, click New, Installed Templates, select Contemporary Photo Album and click Create

 2 This displays sample pages to help you get started

3 Select the Home tab and click the New Slide button to review more than 20 different arrangements of photos and captions, to choose the layout most suited to the specific pictures you want to display

There is tailored support in PowerPoint for photos, as illustrated by the Photo Album templates.

You can replace any of the example photos with your own pictures, and edit the text to provide your own captions.

The Classic photo album contains a similar set of page layouts, but uses rather more sedate black-and-white images to illustrate the options.

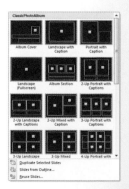

Download a Template

You can download templates from Microsoft Office Online

1 Select the Office button, click New and choose one of the Microsoft Office Online categories

2 For example, Content Slides offers individual slides that can be downloaded and inserted into your presentations

3 Select "More categories", "Name and place cards", then select and download the Numbered Table Tents template

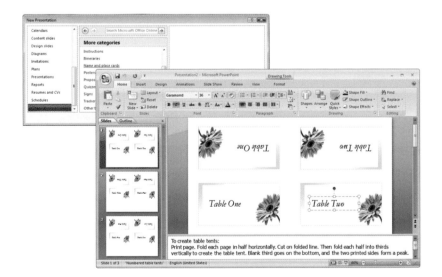

4 Follow the instructions in the notes, to print and prepare the table place tags, making changes to the text as needed

Print the Slide Show

1 Click the Office button, then click the Print button to specify the printer and other printing options

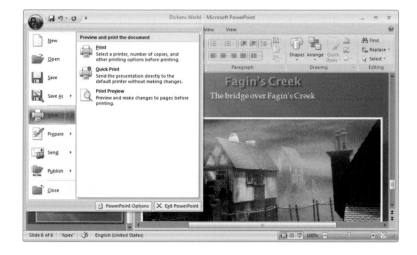

Hot tip

Click the arrow next to the Print button and select Print Preview, to check what will be printed. Select Quick Print to get an immediate print when no changes to printing options are needed.

2 Select the printer and the print range (slides required, by number)

3 Choose what type of document to print

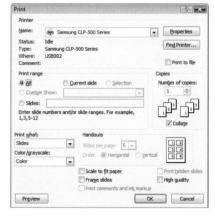

Don't forget

You can choose to print the document in grayscale or pure black-and-white, even if the presentation itself is in full color.

4 If you select Handouts, additional options will be enabled

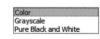

Hot tip

Click the Preview button to see the effect of your selected printing options.

5 Specify the number of slides to a page, and the order (horizontal or vertical). You can also select Scale to Fit Paper, Frames Slides and High Quality

Rehearse Timings

To establish the timings for each slide, you need to rehearse the presentation and record the times for each step.

You can make the presentation easier to run by assigning timings to the slides, so that it can run automatically.

 1 Select the Slide Show tab and click Rehearse Timings, which is in the Set Up group

2 The slide show runs full-screen in manual mode, with the timer superimposed at the top left corner

 3 Advance each slide or animation, allowing for viewing and narration etc., and the times will be recorded

Don't forget

The timer shows the duration so far for the individual slide and for the presentation as a whole.

 4 When the presentation finishes you can choose to keep the new slide timings for use next time you view the show

Microsoft Office PowerPoint

The total time for the slide show was 0:00:59. Do you want to keep the new slide timings to use when you view the slide show?

Yes   No

5 The view changes to Slide Sorter, with individual times for the slides, and Use Rehearsed Timings is selected

Select the Animations tab to make further adjustments to times for particular slides.

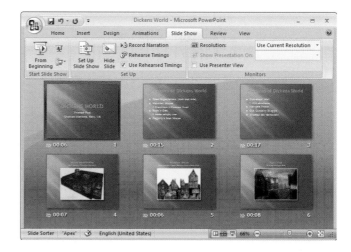

Save As Options

There are several forms in which you can save your presentation.

 1 Select the Office button and click the arrow next to the Save As button

 2 PowerPoint Presentation is the default and saves the presentation in a form that can be changed and updated

 3 Select PowerPoint Show to save in a form that cannot be modified and automatically opens in the Slide Show view

 4 To see what other formats are supported, click the Save As button, then click the down arrow for "Save as type"

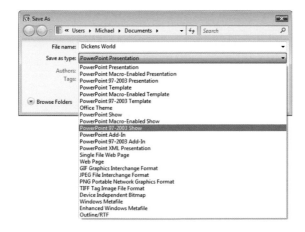

Package for CD

1 With the required presentation open, select the Office button, click the Publish button and select the Package for CD option

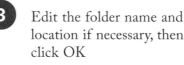

2 Type a name for the package and click Copy to Folder

3 Edit the folder name and location if necessary, then click OK

4 The presentation files are added, along with all the files needed to run the PowerPoint Viewer

7 Office Extras

There are many extras
included with all editions
of Office, including Picture
Manager for editing images,
Document Imaging with its
OCR capability, and Clip
Organizer to manage media
files on your computer. There
are more tools and facilities
available from the Office
download websites.

Office Tools

The Office suite includes a set of tools, as well as applications. Not all the tools will be available, but you can run Office setup to add the ones you want.

Don't forget

Although the option is called Uninstall, it also provides facilities to change or repair programs.

To see which tools are already installed on your system:

1 Select Start, All Programs, Microsoft Office, Microsoft Office Tools for a list

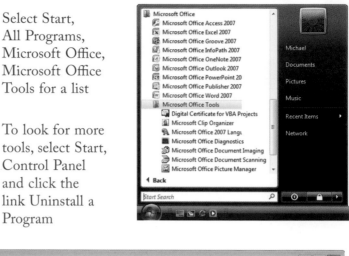

2 To look for more tools, select Start, Control Panel and click the link Uninstall a Program

3 Select Microsoft Office 2007 and click Change

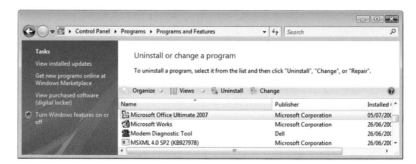

4 Select Add or Remove Features and click Continue

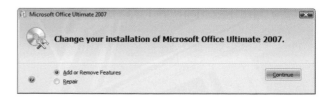

5 Scroll to Office Tools, click [+] to expand the list, click an entry heading and select Run from My Computer

Click a group heading (with [+] or [–]) and choose Run All from My Computer, to add all the tools in that group.

Don't forget

There are also tools in the Shared Features section, which may be selected for installation.

129

6 When you've selected all that you want, click Continue and the programs will be copied and configured for use

7 Click Close to finish setup when configuration finishes

8 New entries will be added to the Microsoft Office Tools folder in the Start Menu

Picture Manager

This tool helps you manage, edit and share your pictures, wherever they are located. It can also provide automatic corrections and adjustments such as red-eye removal.

 Select Microsoft Office Picture Manager from the Microsoft Office Tools folder in the Start menu

 Picture Manager shows the image-file contents of your Pictures folder in the Preview pane

Picture Manager displays the Shortcuts pane and Task pane, as well as the Preview pane. Use the View command to turn these off (see page 131).

If the folder you select contains no picture files, you'll get an appropriate message. For example, when you select Photos:

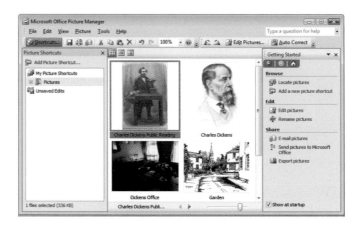

 Click the [+] to expand the folder list and select a folder from within Pictures, e.g. "Photos\Vancouver"

Click the arrow on the Zoom button to select a specific zoom factor, such as 50% of the usual thumbnail size (or of the full picture size in the other views).

51%
800%
400%
200%
150%
100%
50%
25%
12%
Fit

 Drag the Zoom-bar slider to shrink the thumbnails and display more images at a time, or enlarge the thumbnails to display larger (but fewer) images

5 Click Filmstrip View on the Views toolbar

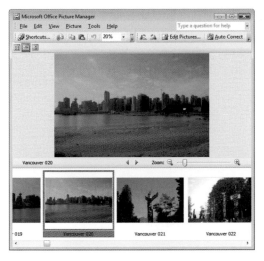

Hot tip

You can change the style of the display in the Preview pane, using the Views toolbar.

6 Click Single Picture View on the Views toolbar

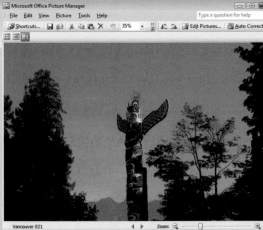

Hot tip

The zoom factor in these views is the size of the main image relative to the full picture size.

7 To close the Shortcuts and Task panes, click the View command and select the appropriate entry to toggle the setting (or click the [x] at the top right of the Shortcuts or Task pane)

Don't forget

The View command also allows you to choose the Preview style and whether to display file names or non-picture-file types.

Edit Pictures

You can adjust the brightness, contrast and color of your pictures, apply red-eye removal, or crop, resize, rotate and flip.

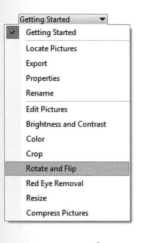
 Click the Picture command on the menu bar and select the function you require, e.g. Rotate and Flip

 Select the picture or pictures that you want to change

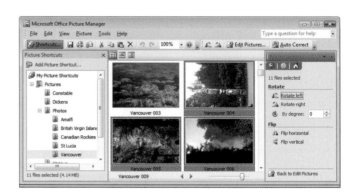

3 Select the subfunction, e.g. "Rotate right" (default 90°)

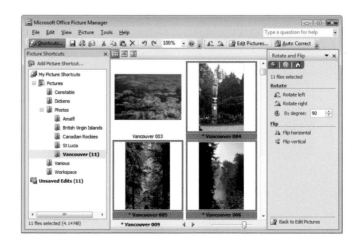

 Right–click Unsaved Edits and select Save All (or Discard All)

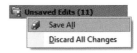

Add Picture Shortcuts

If you have picture files in other folders on your hard disk or on your network, you can add shortcuts to give you quick access without having to navigate the full path.

 Select Add Picture Shortcut (on Shortcuts pane) or "Add a new picture shortcut" (on Getting Started Task pane)

133

Hot tip

Select "Locate pictures" in Getting Started, to search for folders on your system that contain picture files and add them as shortcuts.

2 Navigate to the folder that you require and click Add

Don't forget

You can select folders on any drive on your computer or another computer on the same network (as long as you have authorization to share files and folders).

3 A shortcut to the selected folder will be inserted

Don't forget

You can add or remove folders, paste files or rename the shortcut, and all the changes will be reflected in the actual folder, whether it is on the hard disk or the network.

Document Imaging

With Document Imaging, you can scan both single- and multi-page documents and carry out optical character recognition (OCR). There's a separate Document Scanning component listed in the Start menu, though you perform all operations via the Document Imaging program. For example, to scan a document:

1 Select Document Imaging from Microsoft Office Tools in the Start menu and click Scan New Document

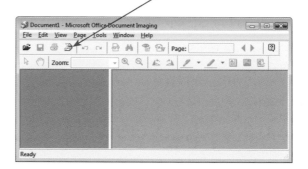

 2 Check the settings, and make any appropriate changes, e.g. color, double-sided or multiple-page documents

 3 Click the Scan button to initiate scanning of the documents

4 Click the Zoom button to see the document close up

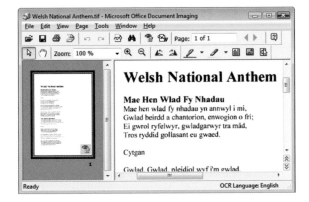

Hot tip

OCR has already been carried out on the document, as you'll see if you click the Recognize Text Using OCR button.

5 Click the Send Text to Word button to see the OCR text

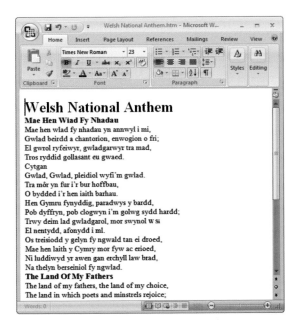

Don't forget

You can use Document Imaging to apply OCR to recognize text in any image document, not just scanned images.

6 Save the document in .docx format if desired

Don't forget

The results of the OCR are displayed in .htm format, but you can save them in a standard Word document.

Language Settings

You may need to work with documents in other languages.

1 This document includes text in Welsh, which confuses the default English (United States) spelling checker

Open the Control Panel, select Change Keyboard, then add the keyboard for that language.

Clock, Language, and Region
Change keyboards or other input methods
Change display language

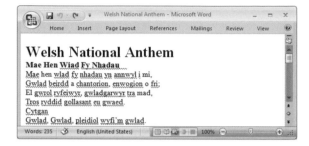

2 To check which languages are enabled and add a new language, click Office Language Settings in Office Tools

Hot tip

Now you can select sections of text and assign the appropriate foreign language.

3 Select the language you require and click Add, and repeat this for each additional language

Clip Organizer

To make use of Clip Art in an Office application, e.g. PowerPoint:

1 Select the Insert tab and click the Clip Art button (or click Clip Art on the Content bar shown on new slides)

This launches the Clip Art task pane, so you can search your clip-art collections. To help you build and manage these collections:

2 Select Start, All Programs, Microsoft Office, Microsoft Office Tools and then Microsoft Clip Organizer

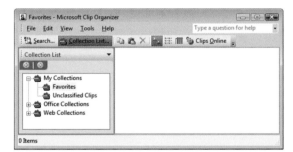

3 Select Office Collections to explore the clip art included

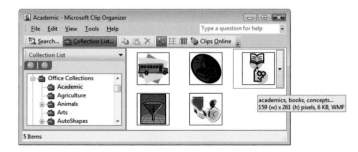

Hot tip

Clip art includes vector images (computed lines and curves), which can be resized without loss of quality. They are used in Word, Excel, Outlook, PowerPoint and the non-Ribbon-style Publisher.

Don't forget

The Clip Organizer in the Office Tools folder provides a separate way of running the same software that's used in the Office applications to find and insert clip art.

Don't forget

The Office suite includes over 400 items of clip art, organized into around 40 categories and described by a series of keywords that can be used for searches.

137

Web Collections

The Web Collections include an entry for the Office clip-art collection available from Microsoft Office Online.

1 Select one of the categories to view the first 100 entries of the typically 1000+ items in each category

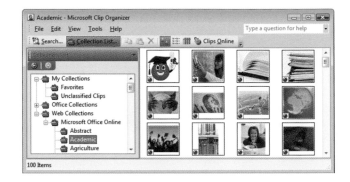

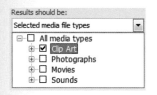
2 Click the Search button, enter one or more keywords and the search characteristics and click the Go button

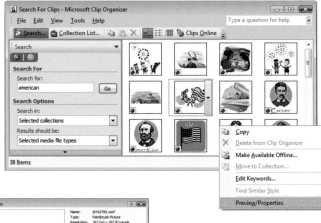

3 Select an item, click the arrow that appears at the right, then select Preview/Properties to see the details, including a larger version

Catalog Your Media Files

To locate the media files on your system:

1 Select File, Add Clips to Organizer, Automatically

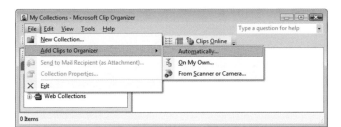

Don't forget

Clip Organizer can manage all the media files on your system, pictures and music as well as clip art.

2 Click OK and Clip Organizer will catalog all of the media files on your hard disks

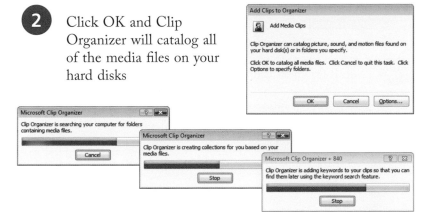

Hot tip

Select Options to choose the specific folders to include in the search for media files.

3 You can now explore the collections that have been added

Don't forget

If there are entries you don't need, right-click them and select Delete. This deletes the Clip Organizer entry only, not the original folder.

Office Downloads

There are additional tools and facilities for Office at the Microsoft website. To find what's available for your system:

The downloads offered will change from time to time, so visit the site periodically to check for the latest features.

1 Go to www.microsoft.com and click the Downloads tab

2 Scroll down to the Browse Downloads by Product section

You can select the Office 2007 tab to see a list of all the applications, but it is helpful to create a customized list.

3 Click the link "Build your list" and then click the button "Autodetect your products"

4 The list is generated; you can select "Save your settings"

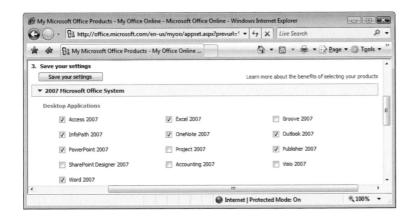

You will be asked to provide your Windows Live email address and password (or to register if you have not already done so).

5 The list shows all your applications that have downloads

6 Click an application, e.g. Word 2007, to see its downloads

Hot tip

The entries will be different for each application but may include items in the Add-ins, Audio, Converters, Demos, Publications, Tools, Updates and Viewers categories.

Get Started Tab

 Click Add-ins in Word 2007 downloads (see page 141) and select the add-in Get Started Tab for Word 2007

 Select Continue to validate your copy of Office

 Select Download and follow the prompts to download and run the installation program for the add-in

4 The Get Started Tab Setup Wizard guides you through the steps to configure the application for the new function

Beware

Make sure that the application is closed, before allowing the setup wizard to apply the changes.

5 When you next start the application, the Get Started tab appears, with its range of training resources

Don't forget

You can download and install similar Get Started tabs for the Excel and PowerPoint applications.

6 Click, for example, "Get up to Speed with Word 2007"

Hot tip

This provides a short introduction to Word 2007. There are other courses and videos available to give further information.

Office System Downloads

see
page 140

1 Display the Browse Downloads by Products section (see page 140) and click the 2007 Office System tab

There are a number of non-application-specific downloads for the 2007 Office system that aren't shown on your customized product list.

2 Select "2007 Office system" to see download categories

Hot tip

When you move the mouse over a command or toolbar button, CLIP displays a translation in a tooltip or window. Translations between French, Alsatian and English are supported. You can also provide your own translations.

3 Select Tools and download, for example, the Captions Language Interface Pack (CLIP), a translation aid

8 Email

The first time you use Outlook you may need to specify your email account. Then you can receive messages, save attachments, print messages, issue replies and update your address book, while protecting yourself from spam messages that might be targeted at your account. You can add a standard signature note to your messages. Outlook helps you subscribe to RSS feeds.

Starting Outlook

If you are running a Windows XP system, you see similar entries, except that Outlook Express rather than Windows Mail is the alternative email option.

Both Windows and Microsoft Office provide email support. To see which is the default email program on your system:

 Select Start, and view the entries at the top of the menu

 Where Microsoft Office Outlook appears as the E-mail option, click this to launch the program

 Where Windows Mail is shown as the E-mail option, click All Programs and select Microsoft Office

This makes Outlook the default, then starts the application. In future you'll be able to select Outlook from the top of the Start menu (as shown in step 2).

4 Click Microsoft Office Outlook 2007, then click Yes

Microsoft Office Outlook

Outlook is not currently your default program for E-mail, Calendar and Contacts. Would you like to make it the default program?

☑ Always perform this check when starting Microsoft Office Outlook

Yes   No

...cont'd

The first time you start Outlook, it takes you through the process of defining an email account.

Outlook detects when no accounts are defined and starts the Auto Account Setup wizard. You can also start this to add additional accounts.

 Choose to configure an email account and click Next

Account Configuration

E-mail Accounts

You can configure Outlook to connect to Internet E-mail, Microsoft Exchange, or other E-mail server. Would you like to configure an E-mail account?

- ● Yes
- ○ No

< Back   Next >   Cancel

 Type your name, your email address and your password

Add New E-mail Account

Auto Account Setup
Clicking Next will contact your e-mail server and configure your Internet service provider or Microsoft Exchange server account settings.

Your Name:	Michael Price
	Example: Barbara Sankovic
E-mail Address:	michael.price33@btinternet.com
	Example: barbara@contoso.com
Password:	*********
Retype Password:	*********
	Type the password your Internet service provider has given you.

☐ Manually configure server settings or additional server types

< Back   Next >   Cancel

Don't forget

You can manually configure your account, but the easiest way to add the account is to let the wizard establish the settings for you.

Configure Server Settings

Don't forget

Your connection to the Internet must be active at this time, so that the wizard can make the connection.

 1 The wizard identifies your Internet connection and establishes the network connection

Add New E-mail Account

Online search for your server settings...

Configuring

Configuring e-mail server settings. This might take several minutes:

✓ Establish network connection
▸ **Search for michael.price33@btinternet.com server settings**
Log on to server

< Back   Next >   Cancel

2 The wizard then searches for the server settings that support your email account

Add New E-mail Account

Online search for your server settings...

Configuring

Configuring e-mail server settings. This might take several minutes:

✓ Establish network connection
✓ Search for michael.price33@btinternet.com server settings
▸ **Log on to server and send a test e-mail message**

< Back   Next >   Cancel

Hot tip

This illustrates the process for the POP3 email account, the standard type. You may need to select the manual configuration for other types of server, using the information provided by your email supplier.

 3 Finally, the wizard logs on to the server using your account name and password and sends a test message

Add New E-mail Account

Online search for your server settings...

Configuring

Configuring e-mail server settings. This might take several minutes:

✓ Establish network connection
✓ Search for michael.price33@btinternet.com server settings
✓ Log on to server and send a test e-mail message

Your **POP3** e-mail account is successfully configured.

☐ Manually configure server settings

< Back   **Finish**   Cancel

 4 Click Finish and your email account will be configured

Your First Messages

Outlook opens with the Inbox showing your first email messages, e.g. welcome messages from the ISP and an Outlook test message.

Title bar   Menu bar   Standard toolbar   Search box   To-Do bar

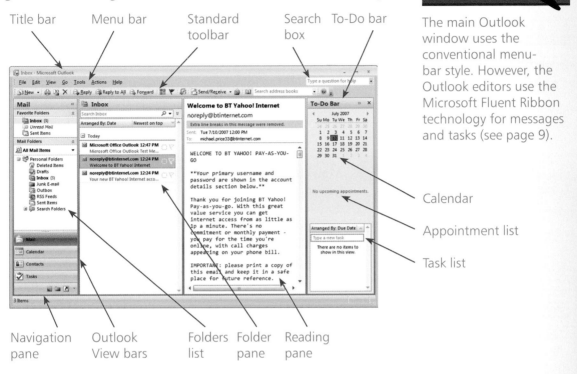

Navigation pane   Outlook View bars   Folders list   Folder pane   Reading pane

Calendar   Appointment list   Task list

You may also receive messages from Outlook of a different type, related to setting up and configuration, for example:

1 Click Yes to synchronize your RSS feeds with the Common Feed List, or click Remind Me Later

2 Click Yes to transfer any existing email accounts from Windows Mail (or Outlook Express) to Outlook

The details for the existing email accounts will be added to the Outlook account settings.

Turn Off Reading Pane

The currently-selected message is displayed in the Reading pane (as shown on page 149). This is a convenient way to scan messages, but has the drawback that messages will be opened even if they are potentially hazardous. To avoid this, you can turn off the reading pane.

Hot tip

It is possible that the very act of reading an email message could release harmful software into your system. Turning off the Reading pane allows you to review the message source and title before it is actually read.

1 Select View, Reading Pane and choose Off rather than Right or Bottom

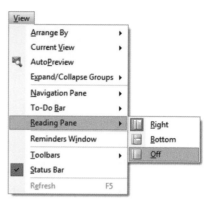

2 Messages will now be left unread until you double-click (or select and press Enter) to open them

Don't forget

Messages are shown arranged by date and shown in groups. You can change the view, for example to sort by sender or subject. When you open a message, you can see that the message editor uses Ribbon-technology function and styling, though there's just a single Message tab in this View mode.

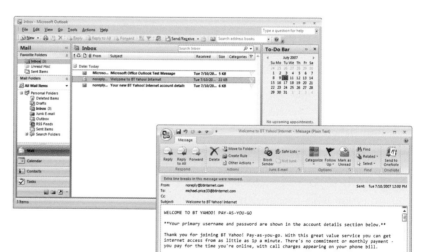

3 When the message has been opened, its entry in the Inbox folder is shown in regular rather than bold font

4 Click the Office button and select Close, or press Alt+F4 or click the Close button to end the display of the message

Request a Newsletter

You'll need to share your email address with friends, contacts and organizations to begin exchanging messages. You can also use your email address to request newsletters. For example:

1 Visit the website www.marshaperry.org/lists

2 Click on the hyperlink "Dickens"

3 Enter your email address, re-enter it to confirm and click Submit

4 Your email address is added to the list and an email inviting you to accept the subscription will be sent

5 Check your Inbox periodically for the message

151

...cont'd

6 Double-click the message when it arrives in your Inbox

7 Select the link provided to confirm you issued the request

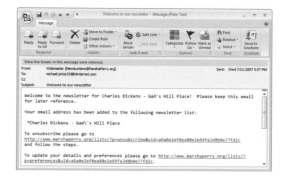

8 Another email will arrive, completing the subscription

Receive a Message

To check for any mail that may be waiting:

 1 Open Outlook, select the Inbox folder and click the Send/Receive button

Send/Receive

2 New mail will be downloaded and displayed in the Inbox

3 Double-click the message title to display the contents

4 Click Other Actions in the Actions group and select Save Attachments, to transfer the attachments to your hard drive

Save Attachments

To save the attachments without opening the message:

 Select the message, then click File and select Save Attachments, All Attachments

File	
New	▶
Open	▶
Close All Items	
Save As...	
Save Attachments	▶
Folder	▶
Data File Management...	
Import and Export...	
Archive...	
Page Setup	▶
Print Preview	
Print...	Ctrl+P
Work Offline	
Exit	

Charles_Dickens_young.jpg
Little_Nell_Journey.jpg
London Map.jpg
All Attachments...

 In either case, the list of attachments is displayed, so you can amend the selection

Save All Attachments

Attachments:
Charles_Dickens_young.jpg
Little_Nell_Journey.jpg
London Map.jpg

OK
Close

 Press Ctrl and click a selected attachment to remove that item, then click OK to download

154

 Locate the folder to receive the downloads (or click Organize to create a new folder), then click OK

Save All Attachments

« Users ▶ Michael ▶ Documents ▶ | Search

Organize ▼ | Views ▼ | New Folder

Favorite Links

Name	Date modified	Type	Size
Dickens Material	7/15/2007 9:20 AM	File Folder	
Dickens	7/5/2007 5:03 AM	File Folder	
Dickens World	7/5/2007 4:52 AM	File Folder	
My Data Sources	6/1/2007 4:15 PM	File Folder	

Documents
Recent Places
Desktop
More »

Folders

Folder name: Dickens Material

Tools ▼ | OK | Cancel

The attachments will be added to the selected folder

Documents ▶ Dickens Material | Search

Organize ▼ | Views ▼ | Slide Show | Burn

Name | Date taken | Tags | Size | Rating

Charles_Dickens_y oung | Little_Nell_Journey | London Map

3 items

Print the Message

1 Click the Office button, select the arrow next to the Print button, then click the Print option

2 You can change the printer or adjust the print settings, for example change the number of copies required

3 Click the "Print options" box to print the attached files as well as the message itself

4 For picture attachments, you can choose the print size (e.g. full page, 4″ × 6″ etc.)

Hot tip

Select Print Preview to see how the message will appear on the page. Select Quick Print to send the message to the printer using all the default settings.

Beware

Each attachment will print as a separate print job destined for the default printer. You can change the printer and the print size on each job, but you cannot combine the prints onto the same sheet.

155

Reply to the Message

 1 When you want to reply to a message that you've just opened, click the Reply button in the Respond group on the Message tab

 2 The message form opens with the email address and subject entered and the cursor in the message area, ready for you to type your comments above the original text

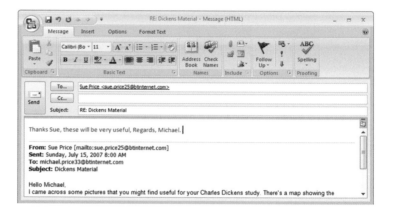

156

3 Complete your response and then click the Send button at the head of the message

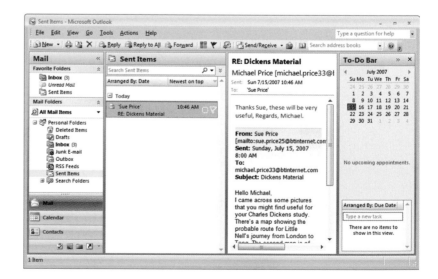

Add Address to Contacts

Whenever you receive an email, you can add the sender (and any other addressees) to your Outlook Contacts list

 Right-click the email address and select Add to Outlook Contacts

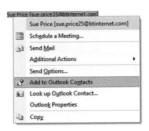

 Add any extra information you have and click Save & Close

Hot tip

You can record a large amount of information, personal or business, for the entries in your Contacts folder.

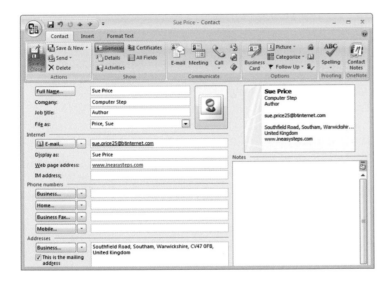

 Select the Outlook folder to create and update entries

Don't forget

Double-click an entry to open it and review or amend the details.

Spam and Phishing

As useful as email can be, it does have a couple of problem areas. Because email is so cheap and easy to use, the criminally inclined try to take advantage of it for their own profit. They'll send out thousands of spam (junk email) messages, in the hope of getting one or two replies.

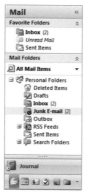

The Junk E-mail filter in Outlook catches the most obvious spam, based on its structure and content and moves such messages to the Junk E-mail folder, giving you a warning message.

To adjust the settings that the filter uses:

1 Select Tools, Options then click the Junk E-mail button in Preferences

2 Select the level of protection: No Automatic Filtering, Low (the default), High or Safe Lists Only

...cont'd

Some spam messages try to trick you into providing details such as passwords, PINs, and validation code. These messages are referred to as phishing (pronounced "fishing"), and are disguised to look like they are from a well-known organization such as a bank, credit card company or charity.

Hot tip

The messages are addressed to "Dear valued customer" rather than to you personally, and imply urgency, so that you'll respond quickly, without thinking.

 Links to pictures on the sender's website may be blocked

 Links to websites may be disabled, and you may not be allowed to use the Reply and Reply All functions

Alternatively, the links may be intercepted in Internet Explorer, with an explanation and caution

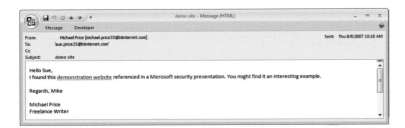

Beware

You can continue to the website, but this is not recommended unless you are absolutely sure that this is not a problem website.

Create a Message

 1 Select the Mail folder and click the New button to open a new mail message form

 **Don't forget**

You can send the message to more than one addressee. You can also select addressees for the Cc (courtesy copy) or Bcc (blind courtesy copy) options.

2 Click the To button to open the address book, select the addressee and click To, then click OK

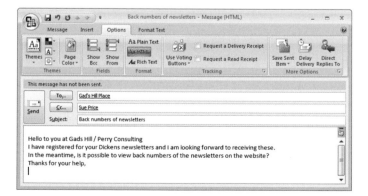

3 Type the subject, greeting and text for your message

Insert a Signature

You can create a standard signature to add to the emails you send.

1 Select the Insert tab and click Signature in the Include group to open the Signatures editor

2 Click the New button, specify a name for the new signature, then click OK

3 Add the text required and click OK to save the signature

4 Now click Signature again and select the new signature to insert it into the message, below the text. For example:

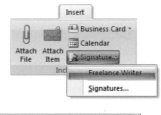

Hot tip

The first time you select the Signature button, there'll be no signatures defined, so you must start off by creating one.

Don't forget

You can specify one of your signatures as the default for new messages or for replies and forwards, and the appropriate signature will be automatically applied for future messages.

161

Don't forget

Click the Send button to store the message in the Outbox ready for sending.

Color Categories

You can use color to help sort and organize your messages.

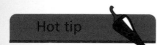
Select the Minimize button to minimize the Navigation pane or the To-Do bar, to make more space for the message properties.

To associate a color with a message:

1 Select the message, click the Categorize button on the toolbar and choose the applicable color

2 The first time you select a specific color, you'll be asked if you want to rename it or assign a shortcut key

Choose Set Quick Click to define the color category to be assigned when you single-click the Categories column.

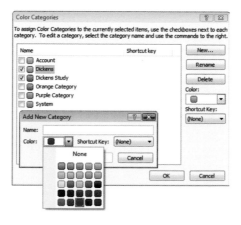

3 Select the All Categories entry to assign more than one color category to a message, or to add, rename or delete the color categories used

RSS Feeds

RSS (Really Simple Syndication) is a way for publishers of Internet data to make news, blogs and other information available to subscribers. You can add feeds and view subscriptions in either Internet Explorer or Outlook. To keep these programs in step:

Hot tip

You may find invitations to subscribe to RSS feeds on websites that you visit or in emails that you receive.

 1 When prompted, click Yes to synchronize Outlook's list with the Common Feed List

2 Click RSS Feeds in Personal Folders for an overview

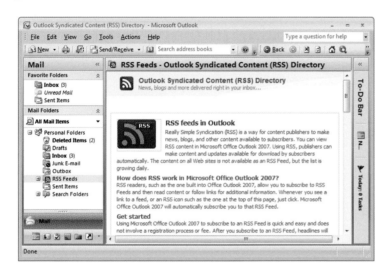

Don't forget

There are some feeds predefined, as indicated by the [+] next to the RSS Feeds folder name.

163

 3 Scroll down to view featured RSS feeds and Office feeds

Don't forget

Select any feed that interests you and Outlook will offer to set up a subscription (see page 164).

...cont'd

Hot tip

Click the Advanced button if you want to change the default options for the feed that you select.

 4 When you select a new feed, you must confirm that you want a subscription

 5 The subscription will be enabled, and the recent history will be downloaded in a subfolder for that feed

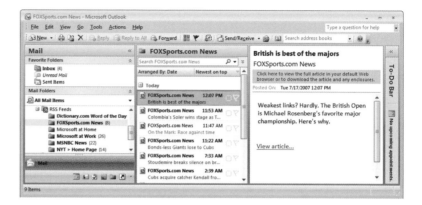

Don't forget

The subfolder will be opened so you can view the latest entries. You'll also see a list of the existing RSS feed subscriptions.

To add an RSS feed for which you have been given the URL:

 1 Select Tools, Account Settings, click the RSS Feeds tab and select New

Hot tip

Copy and paste the RSS feed URL from a web page or email into the input box.

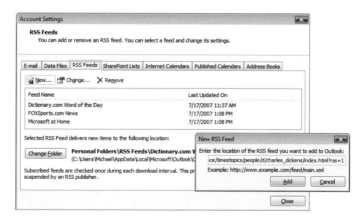

 2 Type the URL for the RSS feed you require and click Add to subscribe and insert it into the RSS Feeds folder

9 Time Management

Outlook is much more than an email manager. It is a complete personal information management system with full diary and calendar facilities. It enables you to keep track of appointments and meetings, and to control and schedule your tasks. You can keep notes, make journal entries and correlate all these with the email messages related to those records.

Outlook Calendar

The Outlook Calendar handles time-based activities including appointments, meetings, holidays, courses and events (single-day or multi-day activities). It provides a high-level view by day, week or month and will give you reminders when an activity, a meeting, or an anniversary perhaps, is due to happen. To open:

1 Click the Calendar button on the Navigation pane

Go	
Mail	Ctrl+1
Calendar	Ctrl+2
Contacts	Ctrl+3
Tasks	Ctrl+4
Notes	Ctrl+5
Folder List	Ctrl+6
Shortcuts	Ctrl+7
Journal	Ctrl+8
Today	
Go to Date...	Ctrl+G
Previous Appointment	Ctrl+<
Next Appointment	Ctrl+>
Folder...	Ctrl+Y

Date navigator   Time bar   View   Events   Meeting

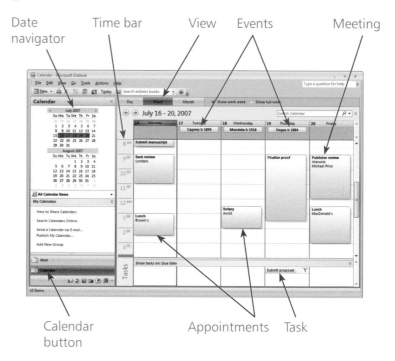

Calendar button   Appointments   Task

You can also view current calendar events on the Today page:

1 Select the Mail button and click Personal Folders

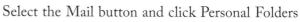

Schedule an Appointment

An appointment reserves space in your calendar for an activity that does not involve inviting other people or reserving resources.

 1 Open the Calendar (day, week or month view) and use the date navigator to select the day for the appointment

If the large Calendar button is hidden, click the small calendar button on the folder bar at the foot of the Navigation pane.

 2 Move the mouse pointer over the time when the appointment should begin, then click as prompted

3 Type the subject, then drag the handle on the lower edge to extend the appointment to the required duration

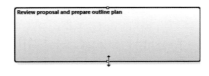

You drag the handle on the top edge to adjust the starting time for the appointment.

Change Appointment Details

You can change and add to the information stored in the calendar.

1 Double-click the appointment to open the appointment editor form showing the information provided so far

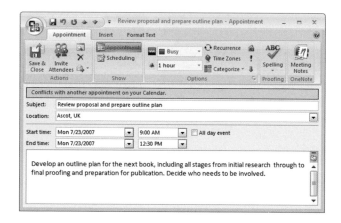

2 Add or change details such as the start time, end time, location or description as needed, then click Save & Close

3 The appointment is displayed in your calendar, alongside any other entries for that time of day

Recurring Appointments

When you have an activity that's repeated on a regular basis, you can define it as a recurring appointment.

1 Open the appointments form and specify the details for a first occurrence of the activity, then click Recurrence

2 Specify how often the activity will be repeated, and over what range of time it should take place

3 Click OK and then click Save & Close to record the changes

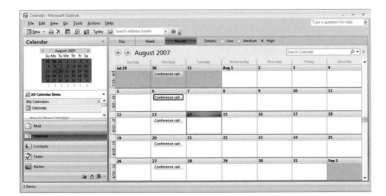

Hot tip

You can take an existing appointment or meeting, and click Recurrence to make it a recurring activity.

Beware

Unless you limit the number of recurrences or set a termination date, the activity will be scheduled for all possible days in the future.

Don't forget

All the occurrences of the activity will now be displayed in the calendar on the appropriate days. If there's room, the recurrence symbol will appear after the subject.

169

Create a Meeting

Hot tip

You can convert an existing appointment into a meeting by defining the attendees and sending invitations.

1 Double-click the appointment entry in the calendar and click the Invite Attendees button in the Actions group

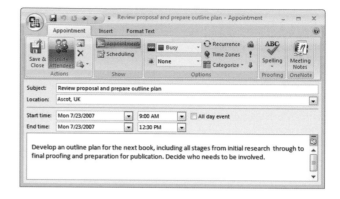

2 On the invitation message form displayed, click the To button to open the address book

Don't forget

You can also schedule meeting resources, such as rooms, screens and projectors.

3 Select the email address for each attendee in turn, and click the Required or the Optional button, then click OK

4 When all the attendees have been added, click the Send button to send the invitation to each of them

5 The invitation will be received as a normal email message

6 The meeting organizer is not required to respond

Beware

The attendees must be using a version of Outlook in order to be able to properly receive and respond to invitations.

Respond to an Invitation

 1 When other attendees receive and open the invitation, it provides buttons to accept, decline or propose a new time

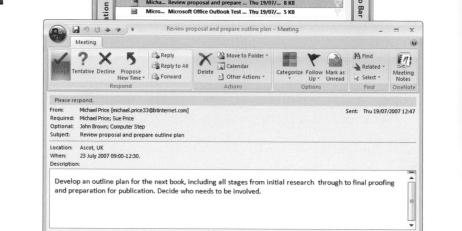

 2 Click Accept, then OK, to send your response and add the appointment to your calendar

3 The original message is removed from the Inbox and the response is inserted into the Sent box

4 The originator will receive the responses from attendees as email messages in the Inbox

Don't forget

The message shows the current status, so it will show the latest information each time it is opened.

5 The message shows the attendee's response and the status

6 The meeting record displays the updated status

Hot tip

Any changes that the originator makes to the meeting details will be sent as update messages to the attendees.

Report Free/Busy Time

Outlook can help you choose the most suitable times to hold meetings, based on reports from the proposed attendees, giving details of their availability.

To publish this information, each attendee should:

Sharing free/busy information relies on attendees and meeting coordinator having access to a drive, a file server on the network or pages on a web server.

 Open Outlook and from the menu bar select Tools, Options

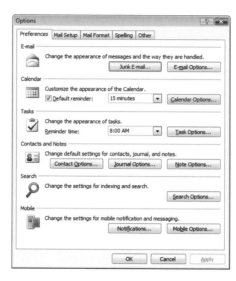

In the Calendar section on the Preferences tab, click the Calendar Options button

 In the "Advanced options" section of Calendar Options, click the Free/Busy Options button

Don't forget

You'd click the Resource Scheduling button to set up a calendar for coordinating resources such as conference rooms and projector equipment.

174

4 Click the box labelled "Publish at my location"

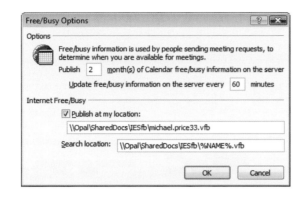

You can specify how much information to provide, and how often to issue updates. In the example, details will be published covering the next two months, and updates will be recorded once an hour.

5 Provide the path to the shared location, in this example the Shared Documents folder on a networked computer

6 For potential meeting originators only, put the same path, but "%NAMES%" as the username to search for any user

7 Click OK to initiate the reporting

Don't forget

The free/busy data is stored in a .vfb file with the file name the same as the username section of your email account.

The files will be stored in the specified location. They will be updated at the specified frequency. To create an immediate update, following major calendar changes for example:

1 From the menu bar select Tools, Send/Receive and then click the Free/Busy Information entry

2 The file is updated and a message will be displayed

Schedule a Meeting

You can use the reported free/busy information to help set up a meeting. For example, to reschedule a meeting you've just set up:

 Open the meeting details and click the Scheduling button

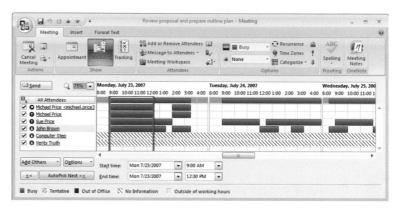

 Click AutoPick Next to see the next available time slot

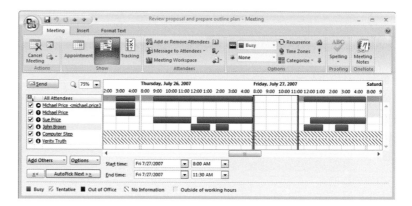

 Click Send to update the meeting and send a message to all attendees showing the changes that have been made and requesting a response

Add Holidays

To make sure that your calendar is an accurate reflection of your availability, add details of national holidays and similar events.

1 Select Tools, Options, Calendar Options (see page 174), then click the Add Holidays button

2 Select the countries that you wish to add

3 Click OK to insert the holidays and events for the selected countries

4 Click OK to exit

5 To see the new entries that have been added, select View, Current View, Events

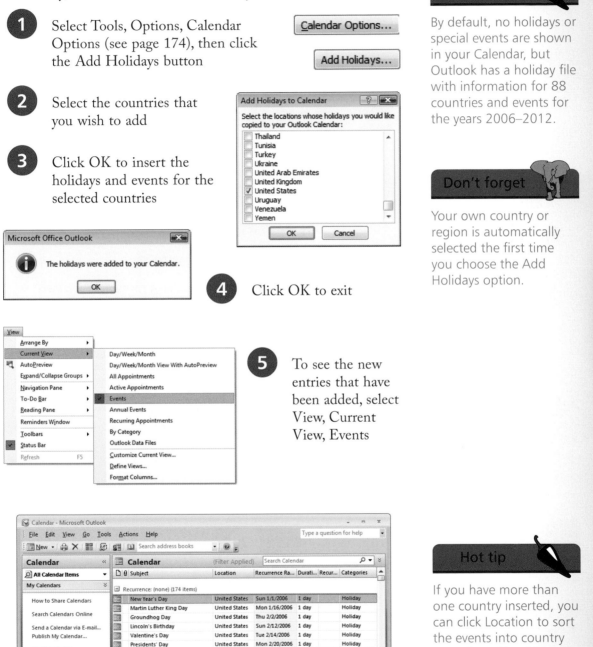

177

Hot tip

By default, no holidays or special events are shown in your Calendar, but Outlook has a holiday file with information for 88 countries and events for the years 2006–2012.

Don't forget

Your own country or region is automatically selected the first time you choose the Add Holidays option.

Hot tip

If you have more than one country inserted, you can click Location to sort the events into country groupings. Use this, for example, to remove events for one country.

Creating Tasks

Hot tip

Outlook can create and manage implicit tasks, which are follow-ups of other Outlook items. It can also create explicit tasks, which can be assigned to others.

To create an implicit task:

1 Right-click an Outlook item (for example a message or contact), select Follow Up and select the flag for the timing

2 The follow-up item is added to the Task folder and also appears on the To-Do bar

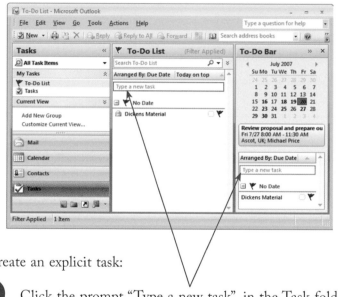

To create an explicit task:

1 Click the prompt "Type a new task", in the Task folder or on the To-Do bar

Don't forget

This provides a quick way to generate a To-Do list of actions. Note that entries change color to red when the due date has passed.

2 Type the subject for the task and press Enter

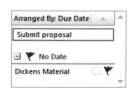

3 The task is inserted with the default characteristics (current date for the start and the due date, and no reminder time)

...cont'd

To make changes to the details for the task:

1 Double-click the task entry in the To-Do bar or Task folder

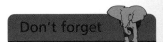

Don't forget

As with the editors for other Outlook items, the Task editor uses the Ribbon technology.

2 You can change the start date or the due date, add a description, apply a reminder, update the priority or indicate how much has been completed

Hot tip

Click the arrows on the "% Complete" box to increase or decrease by 25% at a time, or type an exact percentage in the box.

3 To update the status, click the down arrow and select the appropriate entry from the list

Status: Not Started
Not Started
In Progress
Completed
Waiting on someone else
Deferred

4 Click the Details button in the Show group to add secondary information related to the cost and expense of carrying out the task

Don't forget

Click Save & Close, in Task or Details view, to record the changes.

Assigning Tasks

You can define a task that someone else is to perform, assign it to that person and get status reports and updates on its progress.

To assign an existing task:

 Open the task and click the Assign Task button in the Manage Task group

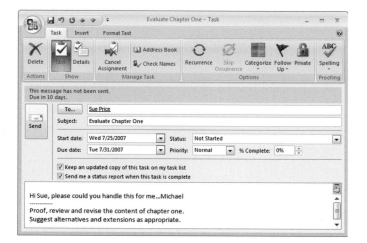

 In the To box, type the name or email address, or click the To button and select an entry from the Contacts list

 Click Send to initiate the task-assignment request, then click OK to confirm the new ownership

 The message will be sent, with a copy stored in the Sent Items folder

Hot tip

To create and assign a new task, select New, Task Request from the menu bar, or press Ctrl+Shift+U. Then enter the subject and other task details along with the assignee name.

Don't forget

Select or clear the boxes for "Keep an updated copy of this task on my task list" and "Send me a status report when this task is complete".

Accepting Task Requests

1 The task details on the originating system show that it is awaiting a response from the recipient of the task request

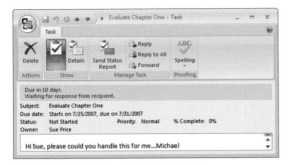

2 The task request appears in the recipient's Inbox

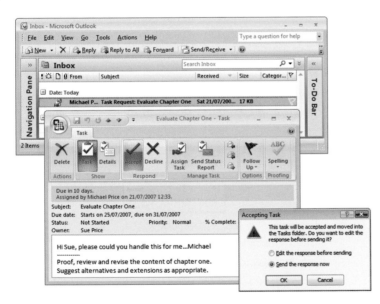

Hot tip

If the task is rejected, ownership is returned to the originator, who can then assign the task to another person.

181

3 The recipient opens the message, clicks the Accept button, then clicks OK to send the response

Don't forget

The task request is sent to the originator, and a copy is saved in the Sent Items folder.

Confirming the Assignment

 The response appears in the originator's Inbox as a message from the recipient of the task request

The originator is no longer able to make changes to the task details, since ownership has been transferred to the recipient.

 When the message is opened, it shows the task with its change of ownership

 The task appears in the originator's Tasks folder, listed under the new owner's name

4 The new owner can change task details, and click Save & Close to save them, as the task progresses

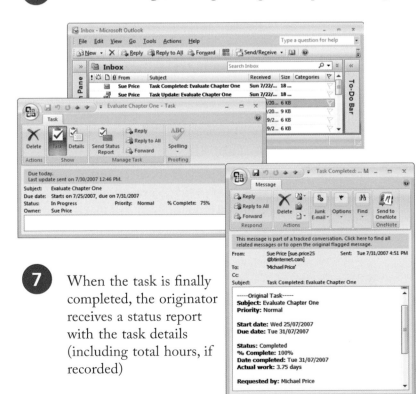

5 When finished, the task can be marked as complete

6 For each change, the originator gets an update message

7 When the task is finally completed, the originator receives a status report with the task details (including total hours, if recorded)

Hot tip

When the recipient makes any changes to the task details, messages are sent to the originator.

Don't forget

Click the message box to list all related messages in the Inbox or Sent Items folders.

Notes

You may need a prompt, but the activity doesn't justify creating a task or an appointment. In such a case, you can use Outlook Notes. To create a note from anywhere in Outlook:

1 Click the arrow next to New on the toolbar and select Note (or press the shortcut Ctrl+Shift+N)

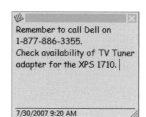

2 Type the text for your note in the form that's displayed, and it will be added to the Notes folder

Remember to call Dell on 1-877-886-3355.
Check availability of TV Tuner adapter for the XPS 1710.

7/30/2007 9:20 AM

3 Open the Notes folder from the navigation pane to see the current set of notes stored there

4 The note titles may be truncated so select a note to see its full title – the text up to the first Enter, or else the whole text if there's no Enter symbol

5   Click Small Icons to allow more space for the note title

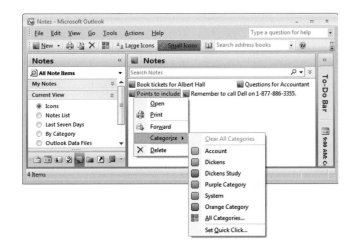

Hot tip

Using category colors, you can associate different types of Outlook item that are concerned with the same subject or topic.

6   Right-click a note to select Categorize and assign a color category to the note

To change the default settings for new notes that you create:

1   Select Tools, Options, Preferences and click the Note Options button in the Contacts and Notes section

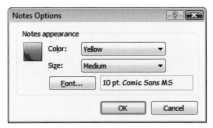

2   You can specify the note color (blue, green, pink, yellow or white), the size (small, medium or large) and the font attributes

These changes will apply to your future notes only – they will not be applied to the existing notes in the Notes folder.

185

Don't forget

Settings offer three sizes of note, but you can click and drag an edge or corner to make a note any size you wish.

Journal

Outlook can automatically record information about activities related to Outlook items in the Journal, a type of project log book.

 1 Select Journal from the navigation pane (or press Ctrl+8)

 2 If Journal is currently not active you'll be reminded of other ways to track activities

 3 Click Yes to turn the Journal on

 4 Select Journal Options for items, contacts and Office file types to be recorded, then OK

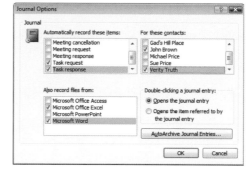

 5 The Journal begins to record the specified data, in a timeline format, as shown in the example below.

10 Manage Files

It is useful to understand how Office manages the files that constitute the documents, so that you can choose the appropriate formats when you share documents with other users.

Windows XP Versus Vista

Despite the visual contrasts between XP and Vista, most operations in Office will be the same. However, file management does exhibit important differences.

Although most features of Office 2007 are independent of the actual version of Windows you are using, there are differences to watch out for when managing files and folders.

To illustrate the variations between the systems:

 Open Word in Windows XP, click the Office button and then select Open

 Repeat the same actions for Word in Windows Vista

This shows the results with Windows Aero. The functionally is similar for Windows Vista Basic but without the transparency effects.

...cont'd

These screenshots show some minor differences. For example:

- The folder for Office document and data files is My Documents in XP, and Documents in Vista

- Access to the drives on your system is via My Computer in XP and Computer in Vista

- Networked drives are found in My Network Places for XP, and in Network for Vista

- XP, unlike Vista, has no direct access to operating-system file and folder search facilities

To see where the documents and computer folders are located:

1 In XP, select Start, All Programs, Accessories, Windows Explorer, then open My Computer, C:, Documents and Settings, the current username and then My Documents

2 In Vista, open Computer, User, current user, Documents

Hot tip

These names are shortcuts to folder locations in the current user profile and to system information about the computer and the network.

Don't forget

In a further change, the Documents and Settings folder in XP is replaced by the Users folder in Vista.

Finding Files

The search facilities are one of the strengths of Windows Vista, and Office 2007 takes full advantage of them. To illustrate this, suppose you've created a document discussing the Stayman bridge convention, but appear to have saved it in the wrong folder. To track it down, when using Office 2007 with Windows Vista:

 1 Open Word and click the Office button and then Open

 2 Click the Search box and type "Stayman"

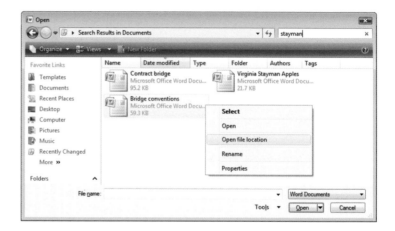

3 Matching documents from the starting location, usually Documents (and its subfolders), are displayed immediately

190

 4 Right-click a file and select "Open file location" to see where it is stored, or double-click to view it in Word

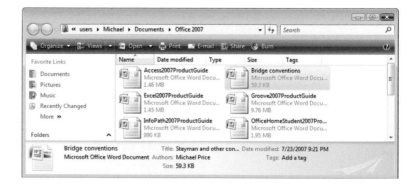

...cont'd

To locate the document when you are using Office 2007 with
Windows XP, you must use the operating system Search facility:

1 Click the Start button and select
Search on the Start menu

2 Select "All files and folders", then specify the file type, a
word from the contents and the location to start from

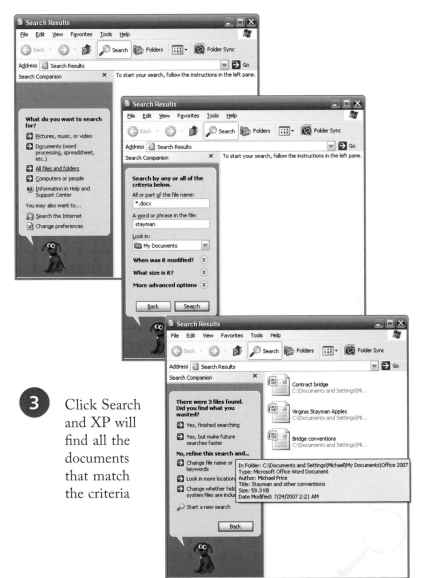

3 Click Search
and XP will
find all the
documents
that match
the criteria

Don't forget

Although Word has been
used for this example, the
same search procedures
apply for documents in
other Office applications,
for example Excel and
PowerPoint.

Beware

In the XP search you'll
need a separate search to
locate documents with
the specified word in
their titles.

Don't forget

Hold the mouse pointer
over a document icon
and the tooltip will show
where the document
is stored.

Recent Documents

When you want to return to a file that you viewed recently, you may be able to select it from the list of recently-used documents.

 Select the Office button and click an entry in Recent Documents to open that document

 To change the number of entries displayed on the list, click the Options button for the particular application

 Click Advanced, scroll down to the Display options, then set the number of recent documents desired and click OK

...cont'd

To change the file types listed when you open documents:

1 Select the Office button and click Open

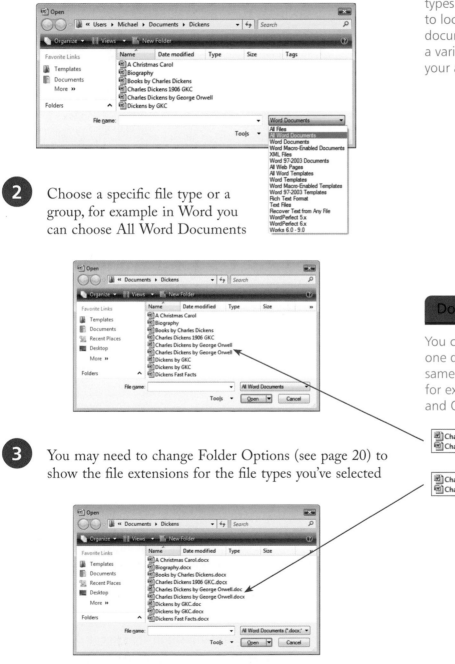

Hot tip

Showing additional file types will make it easier to locate the correct document when you use a variety of file types in your applications.

2 Choose a specific file type or a group, for example in Word you can choose All Word Documents

Don't forget

You can have more than one document with the same name, if you have, for example, Office 2007 and Office 2003 versions.

3 You may need to change Folder Options (see page 20) to show the file extensions for the file types you've selected

XML File Formats

Office 2007 introduces new file formats that are based on XML. They apply to Word 2007, Excel 2007 and PowerPoint 2007. The XML file types include:

Application	XML file type	Extension
Word	Document	.docx
	Macro-enabled document	.docm
	Template	.dotx
	Macro-enabled template	.dotm
Excel	Workbook	.xlsx
	Macro-enabled workbook	.xlsm
	Template	.xltx
	Macro-enabled template	.xltm
	Non-XML binary workbook	.xlsb
	Macro-enabled add-in	.xlam
PowerPoint	Presentation	.pptx
	Macro-enabled presentation	.pptm
	Template	.potx
	Macro-enabled template	.potm
	Macro-enabled add-in	.ppam
	Show	.ppsx
	Macro-enabled show	.ppsm
	Slide	.sldx
	Macro-enabled slide	.sldm
	Office theme	.thmx

The benefits of using the new file formats are:

● Document Size

The new formats are automatically compressed and can be up to 75% smaller, saving disk space and reducing transmission sizes when you send files via email, over networks or across the Internet.

● Document Recovery

Files are structured in a modular fashion that keeps different data components in the file separate from each other. This allows files

to be opened even if a component within the file (for example, a chart or table) is damaged or corrupted (see page 202).

- Macro Management

Files saved using the default "x" suffix (such as .docx, .xlsx, and .pptx) cannot contain executable Visual Basic for Applications (VBA) macros or XLM macros. Only files using the "m" suffix (e.g. .docm, .xlsm, and .pptm) can contain such macros.

- Privacy

Personally identifiable information and business-sensitive information, such as author names, comments, tracked changes, and file paths, can be identified and removed using Document Inspector (see page 212).

Compatibility

To maintain compatibility, Office 2007 can read, edit and save files in the original binary file formats used by older versions of Office. This allows you to create documents in formats that other users can work with, even if they don't have Office 2007.

Alternatively, those users can download the Compatibility Pack:

1 Go to www.microsoft.com/downloads and search for Microsoft Office Compatibility Pack for Office 2007

2 Click Download and follow the prompts to download and install the file-format converters

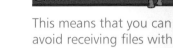
Don't forget

This means that you can avoid receiving files with hidden and unexpected macros that could otherwise potentially affect the integrity of your data.

Beware

For the converters to work, the users must update their versions of Microsoft Office to the appropriate service level:
Office 2000 SP3
Office XP SP3
Office 2003 SP1

Hot tip

With these converters, users of older versions of Office can create, edit and save documents in the new XML formats.

Save As PDF or XPS

There are times when you'd like to allow other users to view and print your documents, but you'd rather they didn't make changes. These could include résumés, legal documents, newsletters or any other documents that are meant for review only. Office 2007 provides for this situation, with add–ins for two file formats.

Portable Document Format (PDF)

PDF is a fixed-layout file format that preserves your document formatting when the file is viewed online or printed, while the data in the file cannot be easily changed. The PDF format is also useful for documents that will be published using commercial printing methods.

XML Paper Specification (XPS)

XPS also preserves document formatting and protects the data content. However, it is not yet widely used. The XPS format ensures that when the file is viewed online or printed, it retains exactly the format that you intended, and that data in the file cannot be easily changed.

Before you can save documents in either format, you must install the appropriate add-in.

 1 Visit www.microsoft.com/downloads and search for "Microsoft Save as PDF or XPS"

 2 Click Download and follow the prompts to begin the installation of the file-format add-in

196

...cont'd

3 Click the Run button and Windows will configure and install the add-in

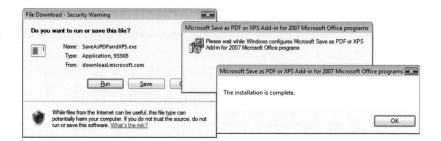

Hot tip

Select Save to download the file to your hard disk, from where you can install it later.

4 With the document open, click the Office button, move to Save As and click PDF or XPS

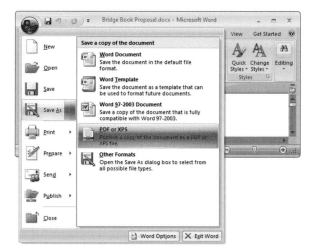

Beware

If you've downloaded a single add-in, only that file format will be made available.

5 Choose PDF or XPS (for dual add-ins), then Publish

Don't forget

You can optimize for online viewing or printing, and you can choose to open the file after publishing.

Fonts in Office 2007

There are a number of new fonts provided with Windows Vista and Office 2007, including Calibri, Cambria, Candara, Consolas, Constantia, Corbel, Nyala and Segoe. You can preview text using these fonts or any of the Windows fonts:

 Select the text to be previewed, then select the Home tab

198

 Click the arrow in the Font box and move the mouse pointer over a Font name to see an immediate preview

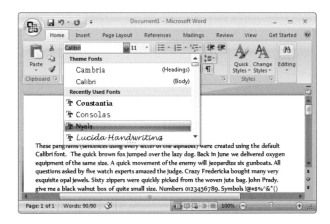

 Click the desired font name to put the change into effect

This helps indicate how the text will appear, but is an awkward way to explore the large number of fonts available.

...cont'd

With the help of a macro available from Microsoft, you can create a document that provides a sample of every font on your system.

 Visit support.microsoft.com/kb/209205

Hot tip

There are two macros. ListFonts creates a document with samples for each font. ListAllFonts provides similar content but in a neater table format.

 Scroll down to ListAllFonts and select the code

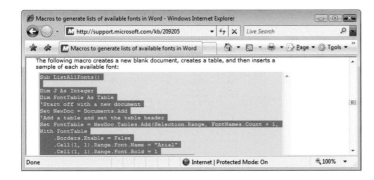

Don't forget

Highlight all the lines of code, ready for copying, from the first line
    Sub ListAllFonts()
to the last line
    End Sub

3 Open a new blank document and select the View tab

Create and Run ListAllMacros

1 Click the arrow on the Macros button in the Macros group and select the View Macros entry

Hot tip

Just clicking the Macros button will select and carry out the View Macros action.

2 Name the macro ListAllMacros, choose "Macros in" Document1 and click the Create button

3 Highlight the skeleton code

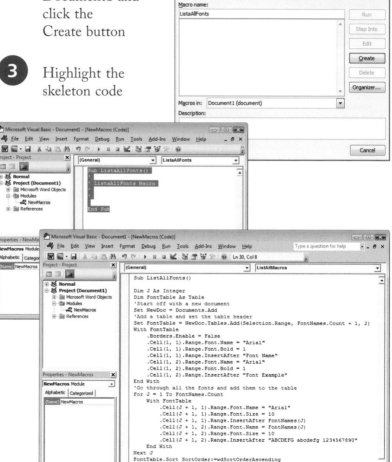

Don't forget

This saves the macro into the current document, ready to run.

4 Copy and paste the code from the Microsoft website, then select File, Close and Return to Microsoft Word

...cont'd

5 Select View Macros again, click the macro name and select Run

6 A new document is created and the font samples are inserted

Beware

The macro is created in the original document, which can be closed without saving. It is not required to view the font samples in the second document.

@Dotum	ABCDEFG abcdefg 1234567890
@DotumChe	ABCDEFG abcdefg 1234567890
@FangSong	ABCDEFG abcdefg 1234567890
@Gulim	ABCDEFG abcdefg 1234567890
@GulimChe	ABCDEFG abcdefg 1234567890
@Gungsuh	ABCDEFG abcdefg 1234567890
@GungsuhChe	ABCDEFG abcdefg 1234567890
@KaiTi	ABCDEFG abcdefg 1234567890
@Malgun Gothic	ABCDEFG abcdefg 1234567890
@Meiryo	ABCDEFG abcdefg 1234567890

Hot tip

You can use your own text for the samples, by changing the code line: Cell(J + 1, 2).Range. InsertAfter "ABCDEFG abcdefg 1234567890"

7 Save the document to keep the list of font samples for future reference

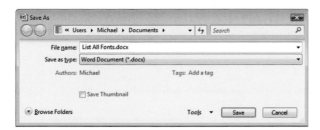

Document Recovery

Sometimes your system may, for one reason or another, close down before you have saved the changes on the document you were working on. The next time you start the application concerned, the Document Recovery feature will recover as much as possible of the work you'd carried out since you last saved it.

1 Open the application (in this case Word) in the usual way

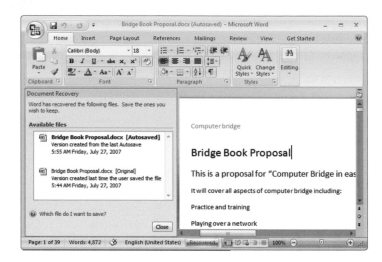

2 View the versions offered and choose the one nearest to your requirement, then save that version

By default, your document is automatically saved every ten minutes, but you can change how frequently this is carried out:

1 Click the Office button, select the Options button for that application, then click the Save entry, adjust the timing and click OK

11 Up to Date and Secure

Microsoft Update makes sure that you take advantage of updates to Office. You can also get the latest information and guidance with online help. Office also enables you to protect your documents appropriately and to secure your system.

Enable Updates

For an application using the Ribbon technology (Access, Excel, PowerPoint, or Word):

 Click the Microsoft Office button and click the Options button for the application, e.g. Word Options

 Click Resources and then click Check for Updates

 You will be invited to install Microsoft Update, which will automatically update both Windows and Office

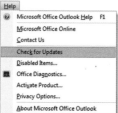

 Click Install to download and install Microsoft Update

5 When installation is complete, you can access Microsoft Update via the Windows Update entry in the Start menu

There's a similar procedure for installing Microsoft Update for Office 2007 running under Windows XP, but in this case a new Microsoft Update entry is placed in the Start menu.

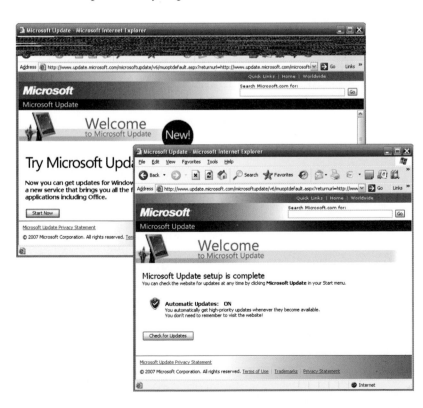

Don't forget

Microsoft Update will run automatically at the set time, but you can invoke the update manually if you want to get your system up to date immediately.

Run Microsoft Update

1 Click Start, All Programs, select Windows Update and click the link Check for Updates

Hot tip

In Windows XP, you'd select the Start menu option Microsoft Update.

2 If updates are found, click Install Updates to apply them to your system

3 You should select all the updates that are marked as important – ten updates for Office in this illustration

Don't forget

Microsoft Update will offer updates only for the specific Office applications that are installed on your system.

4 Microsoft Update will begin installing the updates

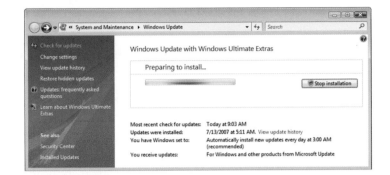

Beware

Sometimes an update may require you to accept the associated terms and conditions before it can proceed.

5 There's usually no interaction required, but you can stop the installation at any time if you wish

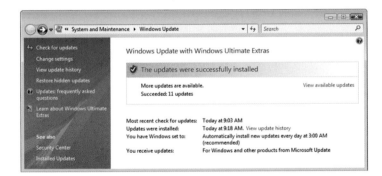

6 Select Office, Options, Resources and click the About button in a Ribbon-based application, or select Help, About for other applications, to see the release level

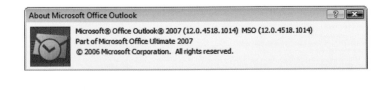

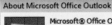

Don't forget

This shows the change in version and release levels for Outlook as shipped and after running Microsoft Update for the first time.

Office Help

There are several ways to display Office Help for an application.

1 Click on the tab row or on the toolbar

2 Press F1 on the keyboard

3 Click Help on the menu bar and select the Microsoft Office Help entry for the particular application (in this case Publisher)

Hot tip

Menu bar and toolbar Help options are provided in non-Ribbon applications such as OneNote, Outlook and Publisher.

208

The Help window that opens is similar for all Office applications.

Back
Forward
Stop
Refresh
Home
Print topic
Font size
TOC
Keep on top

Title bar   Toolbar   Search   Close

Type words to search for

Help topics

Connection status

Status bar

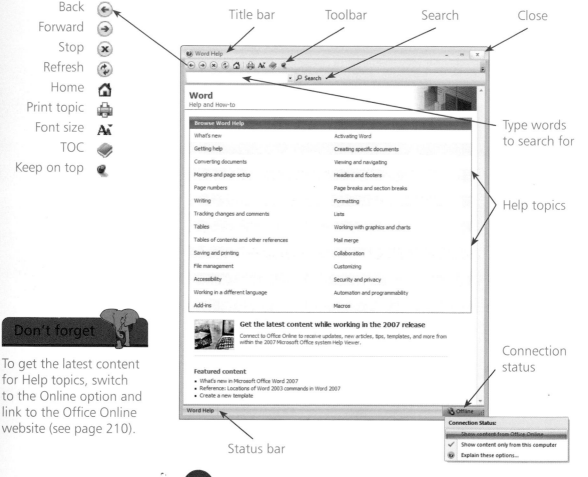

Don't forget

To get the latest content for Help topics, switch to the Online option and link to the Office Online website (see page 210).

4 Click the Connection Status button to change the selected option

Explore Help Topics

1 Click a Help topic to display its list of subtopics, then click one of the subtopics to display the contents

Hot tip

This shows that the topic "What's new" consists of three subtopics. The content is shown for the first of these, "What's new in Microsoft Office Word 2007".

2 Alternatively, click the TOC button to scroll the topics

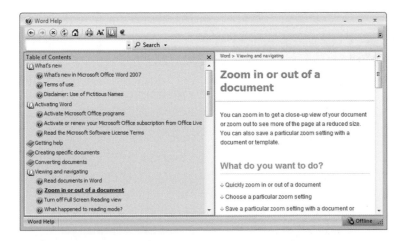

Don't forget

The main topics in the TOC index expand when selected to show the subtopics. Select a subtopic, such as "Zoom in or out of a document", to display its content.

Online Help

The change of connection status will be applied to all Office applications.

Don't forget

With online connection, the topic "What's new" now displays a total of 16 subtopics, including the video training course "Up to speed with Word 2007". Note, also, that the original "Zoom in or out of a document" is replaced by the updated "Zoom in and out of a document, presentation, or worksheet".

Hot tip

In the Help for other Office applications, references to Word 2007 as shown in the illustration are replaced by references to the specific application.

1 Click the Connection Status button and select "Show content from Office Online"

2 If you have the table of contents displayed, you'll see that there are many new or expanded entries available

3 Click the arrow next to the search button to see the range of search areas available offline and online

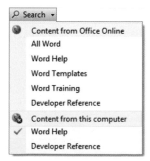

Developer Reference

You'll see that the Search button in Help provides a link to the Developer Reference (in both offline and online versions). This information supports the Developer tab, used mainly by users who will be developing programs and functions for use with Office applications. For this reason it is normally hidden.

However, there are times when it might be useful to have access to features from the Developer tab, for example when you want to record a set of keystrokes as a macro.

To reveal the Developer tab (in Excel, PowerPoint, or Word):

1 Select the Office button, click the Options button for the application and choose the Popular category

Hot tip

In Outlook, you'd select Tools, Options, Other, Advanced Options and then select "Show Developer tab in the Ribbon".

2 Click "Show Developer tab in the Ribbon", then click OK

Don't forget

Enabling the Developer tab for one of these applications enables it in all the other Office applications too.

3 The Record Macro command is in the Code group. The Developer tab also includes the command groups Controls, XML, Protect and Templates

Remove Personal Information

There can be more in an Office document than the information that appears when you review or print it. If the document has been subject to revision, there could be a record of all the changes, including original or deleted text and data. Any comments that reviewers may have added could still be there.

 Select the Review tab and click Display for Review

 You'll see that the file contains the original text, the markup and the final text

Office 2007 makes it easy to completely remove such information.

 Open the document that you wish to publish

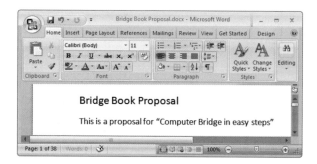

Click the Office button, select Save As and enter a new file name for the document

 Click the Save button to create the working copy

...cont'd

4 Click the Office button, point to Prepare and then select Inspect Document

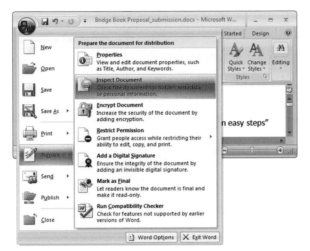

Hot tip

Select those elements that may contain hidden information that you want to remove.

5 Allow headers, footers and watermarks if appropriate

6 Click Remove All to confirm for each item where data was found

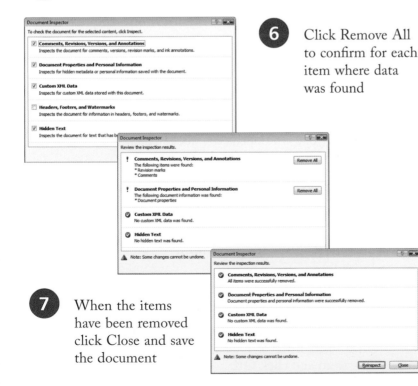

Don't forget

If you've used a working copy, the information will still be available in the original document, just in case it's needed.

7 When the items have been removed click Close and save the document

Protect Your Documents

When you send out a document, you might want to discourage or prevent others from making unauthorized changes. The Prepare function (see page 213) includes several options that will help.

 1 Click the Office button, select Prepare and then click the Encrypt Document option

 2 Provide a password for the document, click OK, then re-enter the password to confirm and click OK again

 3 The contents haven't been altered, but when you close the document, you will still be prompted to save the changes

 4 Now, anyone who opens the document will be required to enter the password and click OK

 5 To remove an existing password, open the document, then select Encrypt Document as above, provide a blank password and click OK

...cont'd

If you simply want to tell users that the document has been completed and should no longer be changed:

 Open the document; then, from Prepare, select Mark Final

 Click OK to confirm and complete the action

3 The effects of marking as final are explained

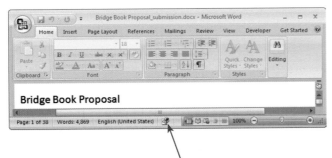

Hot tip

The commands in the groups on the Ribbon are all grayed to show that they are unavailable for this document.

215

4 This is illustrated when you next open the document

5 You'll see the "marked as final" icon in the status bar

Don't forget

Another way to make the document read-only is to publish it using the PDF or XPS document format (see page 196).

6 If you attempt to edit the text, you receive a message

Restrict Permission

If you have the Ultimate or the Enterprise edition of Office, you can go further and apply specific levels of protection.

 From Prepare, select Restrict Permission and then choose Restricted Access

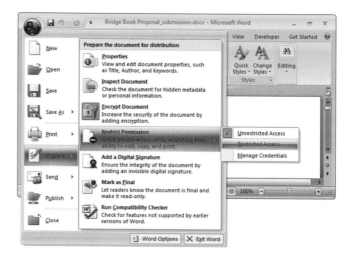

 Sign up for the free trial IRM service

Don't forget

This is a trial service and Microsoft may discontinue it. However, you are promised at least three months' notice of the termination.

 Follow the prompts to register for a .NET passport (or specify your existing passport) and sign in

...cont'd

4 The Windows Rights Management wizard will download an RM account certificate

Hot tip

You can choose a Standard or a Temporary certificate. It is usually more secure to choose the Temporary certificate, especially if there are multiple users on your computer.

```
Windows Rights Management                                        [□][×]

   Completing the Windows RM Account Certification Wizard

      You have successfully downloaded an RM account certificate.

                                                    [ Sign Out ]

   This wizard has downloaded a temporary RM account certificate to the computer. After the certificate
   expires, you can continue to view and use restricted content that is already open on the computer. If
   you want to create or open other restricted content, you must run this wizard again to download
   another certificate. To learn more about certificates, click Help.

   To close this wizard, click Finish.

   Help | Privacy Policy

                        Back        [ Finish ]       Cancel
```

5 Provide the email addresses for users who are allowed to read the document or to change the document

```
Permission                                              [?][×]
  ☑ Restrict permission to this document
  Enter the e-mail addresses of users in the Read and Change boxes (example:
  'someone@example.com'). Separate names with a semicolon(;). To select names
  from the Address book, click the Read or Change button.

  👥 Read...    [                        ]   👥
               Users with Read permission can read this
               document, but cannot change, print or copy
               content.

  👥 Change...  [                        ]   👥
               Users with Change permission can read, edit
               and save changes to this document, but
               cannot print content.

  [ More Options... ]

                                  [ OK ]   [ Cancel ]
```

Don't forget

Anyone wishing to access the document will need to be online to access the IRM service to validate their credentials.

6 Those users must also register with .NET and Windows Rights Management or access is prohibited

```
Microsoft Office Word                          [×]

   ⊗  Cannot use this feature without credentials.

              [ OK ]
```

Trust Center

The Trust Center contains security and privacy settings for Office applications. To open the Trust Center and display the settings:

Hot tip

To open the Trust Center for applications with the menu bar, select Tools and then Trust Center.

1 Click the Office button and the application Options button and then select the Trust Center category

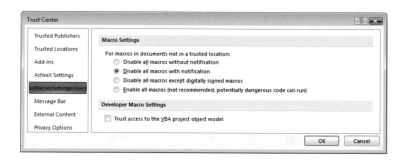

Don't forget

Click the links in the Trust Center to display information about Microsoft support for privacy and security.

2 Click the Trust Center Settings button and choose a category, for example Macro Settings, to see the details

Hot tip

Make changes when required to run macros that you create or that you receive from a reliable source, but restore settings to their original values when you've finished working with the associated document.

3 Select Add-ins to apply more stringent control over these

12 Where Next?

This provides a quick overview of other Office applications that you may add to your edition, and shows you how you can try these products out, by downloading a 60-day trial or by carrying out an online test drive.

Other Office Applications

We have looked at the main Office applications (Word, Excel, Outlook and PowerPoint) and the Office Tools in some detail, and taken a quick preview of Access and Publisher. Depending on which edition of Office you have installed, there are a number of other applications that you might have on your system. The full selection of editions and applications includes the following:

	Microsoft Office Basic 2007	Microsoft Office Home & Student 2007	Microsoft Office Standard 2007	Microsoft Office Small Business 2007	Microsoft Office Professional 2007	Microsoft Office Ultimate 2007 NEW!	Microsoft Office Professional Plus 2007	Microsoft Office Enterprise 2007 NEW!
Microsoft Office Word 2007	•	•	•	•	•	•	•	•
Microsoft Office Excel 2007	•	•	•	•	•	•	•	•
Microsoft Office PowerPoint 2007		•	•	•	•	•	•	•
Microsoft Office Outlook 2007	•	•				•	•	•
Microsoft Office Outlook 2007 with Business Contact Manager				•	•	•		
Microsoft Office Accounting Express 2007				•	•	•		
Microsoft Office Publisher 2007				•	•	•	•	•
Microsoft Office Access 2007					•	•	•	•
Microsoft Office InfoPath 2007						•	•	•
Microsoft Office Groove 2007						•		•
Microsoft Office OneNote 2007		•				•		•
Microsoft Office Communicator 2007							•	
Integrated Enterprise Content Management						•	•	•
Integrated Electronic Forms						•	•	•
Advanced Information Rights Management and Policy Capabilities						•	•	•

For example, if you have the Ultimate edition, that could give you a total of ten application entries in the Start menu, plus the Office Tools and the Office Accounting 2007 Tools folders.

Don't forget

There are also some stand-alone applications (see page 224) that, though belonging to the Office 2007 system, are not included in any of the Office 2007 editions.

Hot tip

There are also Office shared features, such as Clip Organizer and Proofing Tools, that are used within the applications but don't appear as specific entries in your Start menu.

Accounting & Communicator

The extra applications are generally more business-oriented. The main functions and benefits are outlined, to help you decide if any of these products are necessary for you.

Accounting Express

Start - Microsoft Office Accounting

Microsoft® Office Accounting Express 2007

To get started, select one of the following options:

Start a Company

- Set up a new company
- Import data from QuickBooks®
- Import data from Microsoft® Money

Open

- Open an existing company
- Open a sample company

Delete and Restore

- Delete a company
- Restore a backup

Help   Exit

This is a simple accounting program designed to manage finances for the small or home-based business. The Startup wizard gives you step-by-step instructions, and you can import your existing financial data from other programs, such as Excel, Money or Intuit QuickBooks.

Communicator

This helps the members of your group or business to communicate easily with others in different locations or time zones using a range of different communication options, including instant messaging (IM), voice, and video.

The program integrates with other Office applications, including Word, Excel, PowerPoint, OneNote and Groove.

Don't forget

Accounting Express 2007 is available in the US only. Communicator 2007 was scheduled for release after the main components of Office 2007, so it may not be included in your copy of Office.

Hot tip

The tools needed to sell online through eBay and get paid through PayPal are incorporated into Accounting Express.

Don't forget

Public IM Connectivity requires a per-user, per-month subscription license. This application is therefore mainly for use when real-time personal communications form a significant requirement for your business or organization.

Groove and InfoPath

Groove

This program is for working together on a project or report, with a group of people from different departments or organizations. You set up workspaces on your computer and share them with others in the team, and work offline or online, without having to worry about networks or servers.

InfoPath

With this program you can create electronic forms to gather data.

222

InfoPath forms can be sent as email messages, to be completed and returned online. The forms can also be filled in using your web browser. This could be Netscape, Mozilla, Safari and others, as well as Internet Explorer.

OneNote

OneNote

Being included in the Home and Student edition of Office, OneNote is clearly not just for business use. It is intended as a digital notebook that provides a single place in which to gather notes and information. Powerful search facilities help to locate details in the records, and the notebooks can be shared so that you can work with others.

Hot tip

You can search for information from text within pictures or from spoken words in audio and video recordings.

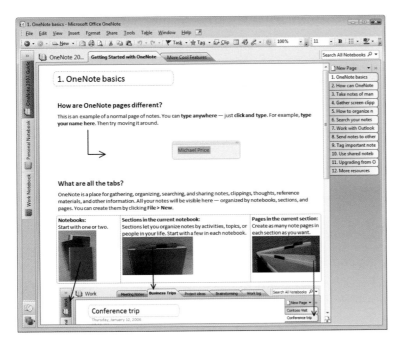

Don't forget

To help you get used to OneNote, there's a OneNote Guide notebook included, which has two sections: Getting Started with OneNote and More Cool Features.

OneNote deals with many forms of information, including text, pictures, digital handwriting, audio and video recordings. It supports two-way synchronization with Pocket PCs and Smartphones using Windows Mobile, so that you can exchange photos, voice recordings and messages.

Although you can run OneNote on any PC, it is especially useful when you use a pointing device, such as a drawing-pad stylus or a Tablet PC pen to add handwritten text or freehand drawings to your notes. You could even use your mouse.

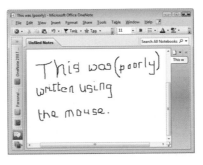

Hot tip

Select Tools, Convert Handwriting to Text to interpret the notes that you have written.

> This was (poorly)
>
> written using
>
> the mouse.

Other Desktop Applications

There are some additional desktop applications that are part of the Office 2007 system but are not included in any of the Office editions. These must be individually purchased, installed and activated. When installed, you'll find them added to the Microsoft Office folder on the Start menu.

Hot tip

You can purchase and install any one of the Office applications not provided with your edition of Office, and it will become properly integrated with all the other Office applications.

Project

This is a specialized product that provides all the software tools and functions you require to manage and control a project. It handles schedules and finances, helps keep project teams on target, and integrates with other Office applications.

Don't forget

The file extension for Project 2007 is .mpp, the same as Project 2000–2003, although the two formats are handled as separate types.

There are two versions – Professional and Standard. Project Professional includes all the capabilities of Project Standard and in addition provides collaborative-enterprise project-management capabilities (these are carried out in conjunction with the Office Project Server product).

SharePoint Designer

This is the web-page and website development product for Office System 2007. It replaces FrontPage, which provided that function for Office System 2003 and previous releases.

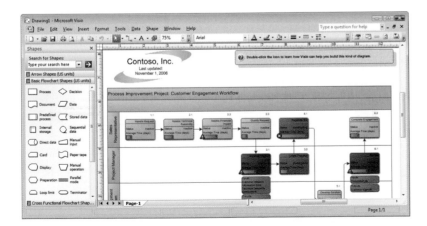

If you have no plans to use SharePoint, you might prefer the Expression Web, which is based on similar technology but without the SharePoint elements. This product is part of the Microsoft Expression Studio group.

Its major strength is support for SharePoint Services, with their emphasis on collaborative working. However, you can still create general websites even if you do not have access to a SharePoint server. SharePoint facilities can then be added at a later date.

Visio

This is drawing and diagramming software to help you visualize and communicate complex information. It provides a wide range of templates, including business process flowcharts, network diagrams, workflow diagrams, database models and software diagrams, and makes use of predefined SmartShapes symbols.

Visio is available in two stand-alone editions: Professional, with advanced visualization features and data connectivity, and Standard, with a subset of the features and templates.

Samples provide Visio diagrams integrated with data to provide context. These will give you ideas for creating your own diagrams and help you decide which template you want to use.

Using MapPoint With Office

While not explicitly part of the Office System, the MapPoint applications can be used with Office applications. The latest editions are at the 2006 level, and there are two main products:

MapPoint 2006 North America

This includes detailed geographic coverage for the United States, Canada and Mexico (cities and major highways only). Other regions are limited to political boundaries and populated places.

Don't forget

There are versions of MapPoint with a GPS locator included, so that the software can be used on a laptop for driving directions.

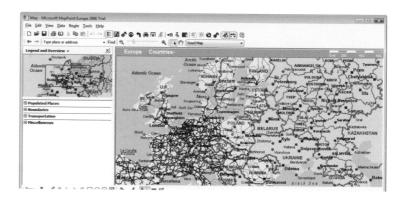

MapPoint 2006 Europe

This provides detailed street-level maps and address finding for the main European countries (e.g. France, Germany and the United Kingdom). Other regions (e.g. Bulgaria, Ireland and Poland) have some street-level coverage but no address finding.

Hot tip

There's a 60-day free trial of these products available on CD or as a download. See www.microsoft.com/mappoint for details.

Order a
FREE TRIAL VERSION
of MapPoint 2006
today!

Working with Office

When you install MapPoint, add-ins are installed into Office applications, so you can use MapPoint 2006 to insert maps into Office documents and presentations directly from the application. For example, you can use MapPoint to insert maps into Word documents.

1 Select the Insert tab, click the arrow on the Object button, then click Object

2 From the object type, select MapPoint Map and click OK

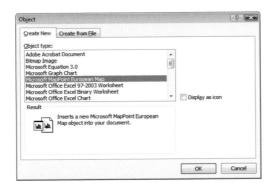

3 The Word user interface changes to include MapPoint options from the MapPoint 2006 program

Beware

You will need to confirm each time you open MapPoint, while you are using the 60-day trial.

4 Click away from the map, and the Ribbon is restored

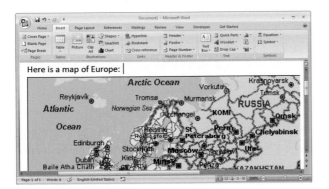

Don't forget

Double-click the map to open MapPoint and redisplay the MapPoint menu bar and toolbars.

Don't forget

The Office server products will require server hardware running Microsoft Windows Server 2003 (or a later version).

Beware

Some InfoPath controls cannot be used if the form has to be hosted on the Forms Server.

Hot tip

The SharePoint Server for Search can be upgraded to the full Sharepoint Server.

Office Server Products

For the larger business and organization, the Office applications can be used in association with a range of Microsoft Office servers. These are intended to facilitate collaboration, help automate business processes and improve management control.

The servers available include:

- Communications Server – provides a standards-based real-time communication platform that supports VoIP call management, audio, video and web-conferencing, instant messaging, and communication between software applications, services and devices.

- Forms Server – provides centralized management of InfoPath forms, allows access out using any browser, including mobile-phone browsers, and provides advanced controls such as "repeating section" and "repeating table".

- Groove Server – for centrally managing all instances of Office Groove in the organization, allowing the use of Active Directory for Groove user accounts, and the creation of Groove Domains with individual policy settings.

- PerformancePoint Server – allows users to monitor, analyze, and plan the business or organization, and includes features for scorecards, dashboards, reporting, analytics, budgeting and forecasting.

- Project Portfolio Server – relates project portfolios to make information available throughout the organization and aid data aggregation, visualization, analysis and reporting.

- Project Server – centrally manages and controls projects, with budget and resource tracking, and activity planning.

- SharePoint Server – supports central storage, sharing and collaborative editing of Office documents, which can be accessed by the associated Office application, by Outlook or via the web browser.

- SharePoint Server for Search – provides the ability to search file-shares, SharePoint sites and websites, and exchange public folders, Lotus Notes databases and customer repositories via protocol handlers.

Trial an Office Product

The functions and capabilities can be quite complex, and you may find it difficult to decide whether a particular Office suite or application will prove suitable for your purposes. However, you can try them out before making your final decision. Most of the Microsoft Office products are available free for 60 days, so you can see for yourself what they can do.

 1 Visit Microsoft's website www.microsoft.com/office and you'll be switched to the Microsoft Office Online website for your location

2 Click the arrow to try the new Office free

Hot tip

If you find yourself at the wrong location, click the location button at the top of the page, then select your location from the drop-down box and click OK.

Don't forget

As well as various editions of Office, you can download trial versions of Accounting, Groove, OneNote, Project or Visio.

3 Click the Try Now button for the product you want

Follow the instructions to register your details, then download and install the product. You'll be provided with a product key that allows you to activate the product for the trial period.

Test-Drive Office Online

The downloads can be large. Even the Home and Student edition will be almost 300 MB. However, you can try out the products without downloading them.

 Click the arrow to try the new Office free (see page 229) and then click the link to "Test it out in your browser"

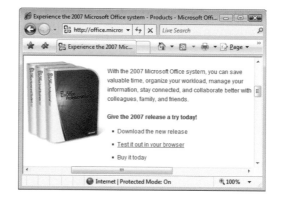

(see page 229)

 Click "Test Drive Microsoft Office"

 Agree to load the Citrix browser plug-in if requested   Load Citrix Browser Plug-in

4 Click the Register Now link and sign up for a Windows Live ID (or sign in using your existing ID)   Register Now

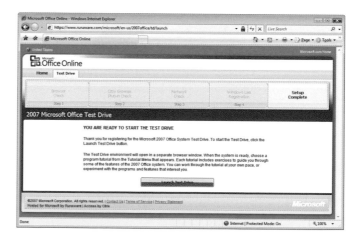

...cont'd

5 Click the link to Launch Test Drive

6 The Citrix program opens a new Internet Explorer window and sets up the evaluation environment and the tutorials

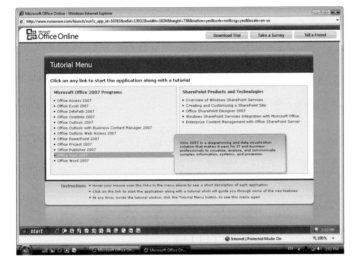

The trial versions hosted in the test drive contain most of the functionality of the regular versions, but saving and printing of documents is not enabled.

7 Select an application to try it out using the tutorial

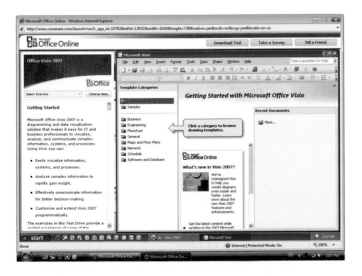

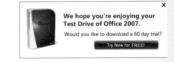

You'll be given a reminder to download a 60-day trial, if you wish.

We hope you're enjoying your **Test Drive of Office 2007.**
Would you like to download a 60 day trial?
Try Now for FREE!

Office Newsletters

 1 At office.microsoft.com click the Help and How–to tab

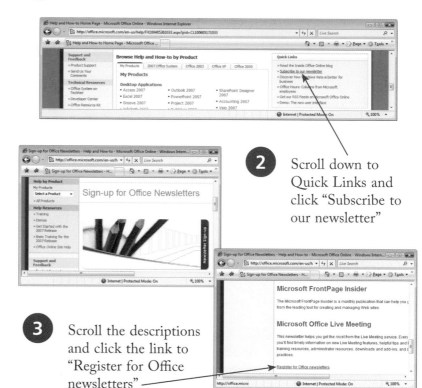

2 Scroll down to Quick Links and click "Subscribe to our newsletter"

3 Scroll the descriptions and click the link to "Register for Office newsletters"

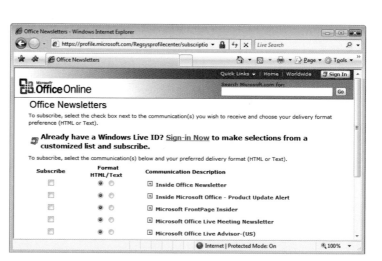

4 Select the newsletters that you'd like to receive

Index

Symbols

A

B

C

P

U

V

W

X

Y

Z